JOHN WHITE

Putting the Soul Back in Psychology

When Secular Values
Ignore Spiritual Realities

INTERVARSITY PRESS
DOWNERS GROVE, ILLINOIS 60515

The Pascal Lectures on Christianity and the University

Malcolm Muggeridge, *The End of Christendom,*
October 1978 (Eerdmans, 1980)
Donald MacKay, *Science and the Quest for Meaning,*
October 1979 (Eerdmans, 1982)
Charles Malik, *A Christian Critique of the University,*
March 1981 (InterVarsity Press, 1982)
Josef Pieper, *What Is a Feast?*
November 1981
John White, *Putting the Soul Back in Psychology,*
March 1983 (InterVarsity Press, 1987)
Alvin Plantinga, *Faith, Reason and Freedom,*
March 1984
Madeleine L'Engle, *Poppy Flower Sandwiches,*
October 1984
Colin Russell, *Science and Apocalypse,*
March 1986

InterVarsity Press is the book-publishing division of InterVarsity Christian Fellowship, a student movement active on campus at hundreds of universities, colleges and schools of nursing. For information about local and regional activities, write Public Relations Dept., InterVarsity Christian Fellowship, 6400 Schroeder Rd., P.O. Box 7895, Madison, WI 53707-7895.

Distributed in Canada through InterVarsity Press, 860 Denison St., Unit 3, Markham, Ontario L3R 4H1, Canada.

Cover illustration: Roberta Polfus

ISBN 0-87784-979-X

Printed in the United States of America

Library of Congress Cataloging in Publication Data

White, John, 1924 Mar. 5-
   Putting the soul back in psychology.

   Bibliography: p.
   1. Christianity—Psychology.   2. Psychology—
Religious aspects—Christianity.   I. Title.
BR110.W455   1987   261.5'15   86-27302
ISBN 0-87784-979-X

17	16	15	14	13	12	11	10	9	8	7	6	5	4	3	2	1
99	98	97	96	95	94	93	92	91	90	89	88	87				

Preface

Some years ago it was my privilege to deliver the Pascal Lectures in Waterloo University. I chose to discuss the human encounter with God. In the first lecture I contrasted theistic and humanist understandings of Man, and in the second, the problem of how I being finite could encounter Infinity, being matter could encounter Spirit, or being sinful could encounter Holiness. I addressed the questions as a convinced Christian and as a psychiatrist.

I was also asked to meet with the faculties of psychology and theology to discuss these issues informally. The substance of the four occasions (two academic lectures and two informal discussions) makes up the four chapters of this book. In chapters one and four the Pascal lectures are retained much as they were delivered. Chapters three and four arise out of the discussions in the faculties of psychology and theology. These have been revised extensively and new material added.

I challenged members of the faculty of psychology to abolish taboos about religious material, to be less arrogant in dealing with religious clients and to stop denying their own essentially religious nature. Psychology's view of Man was seriously defective. In any case winds of change blowing out of California threatened to sweep away in a decade a system of thought that had taken thousands of years to develop. Psychology was *already* succumbing to religion. But did it have to be a potted, half-baked understanding of the religious East?

In the theological faculty I deplored theology's tendency to sell out to the human sciences, to exchange treasure for a mess of pottage. I could not hide the sense of betrayal and alarm I felt that those to whom I looked for a better understanding of my faith were tasting the latest tidbits from my own area of expertise, sometimes finding more significance in them than in revelation.

In this book, then, I am trying to face the most basic issue of all in psychology: Who and what are we? Unless the question is faced squarely and repeatedly, psychological help will never achieve what it sets out to. Superficially "Christianized" versions of psychology will likewise not help. To mend a watch one must have two kinds of understanding. First, we must know how the mechanism works, and second, the purpose of the instrument itself. Someone who had no concept of time or who attached no importance to it might grasp the mechanics and electronics of a watch perfectly, but would have serious problems setting the time. This is precisely the nature of the difficulty facing both psychologists and Christian counselors today. It is time we faced it.

ONE

MORE HUMAN THAN HUMANISTS KNOW

Who are we?

We have always had a fascination with ourselves. Some inner insecurity or curiosity compels us to answer what it means to be human—or better, what it means to be uniquely human. Is it our ability to use tools? Some animals have been shown to fabricate primitive tools. Is it our ability to think? Some machines are very close to imitating human thought. And scientists tell us it is not a question of *if* we will create computers that think, but *when*.

This book will by no means offer a complete answer to this question. But I invite you to join me in exploring some possibilities. There are many places we could start. But let me begin, as a partial answer, by comparing and contrasting the views of contemporary scientific humanism with those of the Judeo-Christian tradition.

The Cracked Mirror

The views of both perspectives could be summarized with the image of a cracked mirror. A cracked mirror gives a distorted image. When I look at my face in a badly broken mirror, I might laugh, feel annoyed or become whimsical at the absurd distortion confronting me. Both the Judeo-Christian tradition and scientific humanism are preoccupied with the duality of our nature—the good and the evil, the noble and the reprehensible. How can it be that there is so much to marvel at in us and at the same time so much that is despicable? We may display a love of both justice and mercy, and be capable of loyalty, affection and love—even to the point of self-sacrifice. Yet we are also capable of committing unspeakable atrocities.

A cracked mirror reflects certain parts of our faces accurately. It cannot altogether conceal the handsomeness of a man or the beauty of a woman. But neither can it reveal them fully. The image confronting us may be comical, sinister or even in some bizarre fashion both of these.

To change the metaphor, human glory is like the glory seen in a truncated Greek sculpture. You can still admire what you see. But tragedy has overtaken the sculpture, tragedy for which no remedy can be found. While we are glad to display it in a gallery, we lament something irreplaceable that time, catastrophe or vandalism has robbed us of.

Neither the Judeo-Christian perspective nor the humanist world view is monolithic. Christians differ with one another. Jews quarrel with Jews. And humanists, perhaps with a little less hostility, by no means agree about the essence of their system of thought. More confusing yet, many people who proudly assert their Christianity or their Semitism think like scientific humanists when they get down to explaining their views about human nature.

When, therefore, I refer to the Judeo-Christian (or theistic) view of what is human, I refer to the contents of the historical documents common to Jews and Christians. In the case of Jews I am thinking of the five books of Moses, the records of Israel's history at least up to the time of Nehemiah and the return of the Jews from captivity, the Wisdom literature (books like the Psalms and Proverbs) and the writings of the prophets. In the case of Christians I refer to the early records of the life and sayings of Jesus, and to the correspondence of first-century church leaders—those documents that now comprise what we call the New Testament. I maintain that whatever may be the behavioral inconsistencies of both Jews and Christians, the view of human nature throughout these documents is remarkably consistent.

Now Jews and Christians have their Scriptures, but what shall I say of humanists? We have the art and the writings of Christian humanists during the Renaissance, the works of the later deistic humanists, and more recently Humanist Manifesto I (1933) and Humanist Manifesto II (1973). From the manifestoes, but more from the widespread scientific view of who we are, I wish to focus only on what is said about evolutionary origins.

Let me make a further clarification. As a Christian I have

no question about the superiority of the theistic view over the humanist view. I shall even give some of my reasons for rejecting the view of the scientific humanists. But I do not know whether to laugh or to cry about the recent attacks on humanism by members of the religious right wing. Curt Sytsma has parodied the issue rather well in his amusing verses.

In every age the bigot's rage
Requires another focus;
Another devil forced on stage,
By hatred's hocus-pocus:

The devil used to be a Jew
And then it was the witches;
And then it was the Negroes
Who were digging in the ditches.

The devil once was colored pink
And labelled communistic:
Now all at once, in just a blink,
The devil's humanistic.

We cannot place all the blame for promiscuity, the increase in sex crimes, in the divorce rate and in the abortion rate on humanists, even though their ideas have been a contributing factor. As David Neff has pointed out, the vast social changes that have overtaken us during the last fifty years or so owe much more to the mass production of automobiles than to humanist influence.[1]

One last word before I begin in earnest. From time to

time I will use the word *Man,* spelled with a capital M, to mean the *human being,* whether male or female. *Man* is easier to say and write than *the human being.* Whether we like it or not, we are stuck to some extent with what some people might view as a language containing innate sexism. A writer who tries to be linguistically nonsexist, finds herself or himself saying him or her, his or hers, or pluralizing hers or his personal pronouns to a nonsexist *they.* I hope you will accept me as a nonchauvinist and permit me to use the term *Man* in a generic sense occasionally.

The Humanist View

As I mentioned before, humanists, Jews and Christians all see good and evil, the noble and the despicable in human beings. Some humanists dislike the term *sin,* but they all recognize human flaws and brokenness. Certainly I see in the attitudes of humanists (including those of my fellow psychiatrists) the same judgmental and hostile attitudes that some Christians display toward the sins of others. But let me turn to the nub of the issue.

Humanists see Man as supreme because he stands at the pinnacle of evolutionary development. They see in Man a supreme creature who has risen from below. We might entitle his story "The Ascent of the Naked Ape." We rose to our pinnacle because of our large brains and our manual dexterity. We use a large and complex set of symbols to communicate. We have for millennia stored vital information in and retrieved it from great libraries. Our ascendancy lies in these qualities and in the civilizations that have arisen from them.

And in these civilizations humanists see our greatest glory—in our creativity, in the nobility of our architecture, our paintings, our music, our writings and our philosophizing. Theists, as we shall see in a moment, differ from humanists here.

In their abhorrence of certain evils, however, scientific humanism and the Judeo-Christian tradition are united. Both systems reject violence and war. Both deplore dishonesty and the exploitation of the weak by the strong. But again as we shall see in a moment, the Judeo-Christian tradition deplores many other kinds of human behavior acceptable to humanists.

The disagreements arise from the fundamental difference in their respective understandings of human nature, of our origins and of the total environment in which we find ourselves. For an understanding of human evil the humanist must look to evolution. Arthur Koestler, the novelist whose suicide not long ago startled the literary world, devoted a trilogy to the subject (*The Sleepwalkers, The Creative Act* and *The Ghost in the Machine*). Koestler claimed neurological evidence suggested that the explosive growth of the human brain has resulted in faulty coordination between phylogenetically primitive and more recent brain structures.

In the preface to the third book he tells us that "the creativity and the pathology of the human mind are, after all, two sides of the same medal coined in the evolutionary mint. The first is responsible for the splendor of our cathedrals, the second for the gargoyles that decorate them to remind us that the world is full of monsters, devils and succubi. They reflect the streak of insanity which runs through the history of our species, and which indicates that somewhere along the line of its ascent to prominence something has gone wrong."[2] Koestler's solution? Some kind of chemical to make our brains work properly and to bring us universal peace. Not all humanists agree with Koestler, but all do look to an evolutionary hypothesis for the source of the evil and for some solution to the problem.

Three Problems

Three problems concern me with the humanist view:

1. Its idea of our nobility.
2. Its optimism.
3. Its essentially deterministic view.

First, let us examine the issue of our nobility. Humanists have a point when they see nobility in the works of our hands and brains. Let us be slow to cavil. The Seven Wonders of the ancient world do in fact startle us. And wonders, those wonders human beings create in the modern world, do the same. Men have gone to the moon and returned alive. The complexity of our technological sorceries stuns and awes us. I sing to my Amiga computer and it responds to me, graciously and sycophantically providing an orchestrated background to my croaks and wheezes. I sing louder and the accompaniment swells to support me. I increase the tempo and, sensitive to my every cue, it quickens the pace of the accompaniment. What kind of species do I belong to that can design such a flattering marvel—a marvel which will be superseded tomorrow or the next day?

Will I ever be able to absorb the incredible richness of even one major art gallery, or ever digest the musical subtleties of my own record collection, or the wisdom and passion contained in the books on my bookshelves? And has the world ever seen an artistic outpouring comparable with

that of the end of the twentieth century? Such stunning ath-
letic performances? The dedication, the energy, the courage,
the relentless pursuit of excellence compels our response.

Of course we must not confuse quantity with quality. I am
awed as much by Inca masonry and by ancient Chinese
calligraphy as by the latest flood of violin performances or
film productions. We have advanced technologically, but the
ancients did more with less, and we are only building on
their foundations. If we are great, then we have been great
for millenia.

But before we indulge in worshiping the images in our
mirrors, we must ask the question, In what does that nobility
lie? And is it in fact an evolutionary product? For we have
been artistic and creative since we lived in caves. G. K.
Chesterton makes wry comments about the cave man or
cave woman who created the beautiful pictures on the walls
of a now famous (if somewhat inaccessible) cave in France.
He contrasts the popular picture of the cave man—club-in-
hand, brutal, fearful, sexually aggressive—with the actual
cave artist's sensitivity and the kindly but accurate observa-
tion he must have possessed to do the paintings. The cave
was not, Chesterton said, "a Bluebeard's chamber filled with
the skeletons of slaughtered wives; it was not filled with
female skulls all arranged in rows and cracked like eggs. It
was something quite unconnected . . . with all modern
phrases and philosophical implications and literary rumors
which confuse the whole question for us."

Chesterton continues, "When the realist of the sex novel
writes, 'Red sparks danced in Dagmar Doubledick's brain;
he felt the spirit of the cave man rising within him,' the
novelist's readers would be very much disappointed if Dag-

mar only went off and drew large pictures of cows on the drawing room wall."³

We all agree that we are noble, or, with more humility, that we belong to a noble race. But where did the nobility come from? And when did it first appear? Is it possible that we are confusing creativity and nobility with sophistication? Having drawn pictures based on skeletons, have we looked at them and concluded, "Nothing noble or creative could ever come out of *that*"? (After all, as a middle-aged, middle-class male I used to react to the hairiness and smell of hippies pretty much as I would react to pictures of cave men. They didn't *look* noble.) What evidence is there that the creatures we depict lacked nobility? The evidence we have suggests the contrary.

But let me ask another question. Suppose we put the matter the other way round. Is there any evidence at all that we are growing more noble? After all, evolution is an amoral process selecting the fittest for survival. There is no reason to suppose that it could produce nobility—a characteristic which even today can get you put in jail or shot. Who, for example, would want to go to Russia and become a truly creative artist or poet? Nobility and creativity would seem to be evolutionary disadvantages.

Second, there is a problem with the optimism of the humanistic perspective. The theistic view of Man is much grimmer about the evil in us, seeing it as both the source and the consequence of humanity's greatest catastrophe. It is not easy to be optimistic about our future these days. What hope is there for our planet? We do not know. We can only hope, pray and engage in what many Jews, Christians and humanists are united in doing—devoting every effort to avert a nuclear holocaust.

And who dares to be confident about the outcome? I suspect that any optimism about our growth in nobility represents little more than wishful thinking, a bed to hide under as the specter of nuclear world war approaches us.

Scientific humanism has never truly weighed the terrible power of evil in us all. It is dangerous to underestimate an enemy's strength, and the danger was never greater than now.

Third, I have a problem with humanism because it is deterministic. Now many humanists might feel this characterization is unfair. Don't they believe in Man's ability to control his own destiny? Many do. But I believe they have failed to seriously consider some of their key premises.

Determinism is a term given to the view that the universe is a closed system governed by the laws of cause and effect and by the random associations of chance. There is nothing outside the universe that can affect or change it. Only what is inside the material universe matters. More to the point, human beings are seen as closed systems.

The human sciences approach human behavior in the same way that physicists and chemists explore the physical universe. Psychoanalysis and behaviorism, the classical psychological sciences, share the same basic assumptions. Our behavior is predeterminable, predictable. There are no forces outside observable laws and factors that can change us. That is why scientific investigation is possible. Our sense of voluntary choice is illusory. We may think we make choices every day of our lives, but we fool ourselves. Spontaneity does not exist.

Those of us who practice psychotherapy tend to close our

minds to the implications of this. Our patients may be closed systems, reacting to our therapeutic strategies with the same balancing mechanisms that govern the lives of simple cells while we in our wisdom supervise the process, administering stimuli from time to time. But we fool ourselves, for we are the same as our clients. And we are doubly fools, failing to see you can't think logically in a closed system.

Both J. B. S. Haldane and C. S. Lewis pointed it out. Haldane said, "If my mental processes are determined wholly by the motions of atoms in my brain, I have no reason to suppose that my beliefs are true . . . and hence I have no reason for supposing my brain to be composed of atoms."[4]

Lewis's argument is more extensive. He concludes that *naturalism* (a name he gives to what I have been calling scientific humanism) is forced to concede that "all thoughts whatever are . . . the results of irrational causes, and nothing more than that. The finest piece of scientific reason is caused in just the same irrational way as the thoughts a man has because a bit of bone is pressing on his brain. . . . Both are equally valueless."[5]

Could B. F. Skinner be one of the few humanists to see it? Not many of us like his solution. Yet he is at least consistent. Since the human organism is a closed system, he suggests we treat it like one, strip it of its dignity and condition the evil out of it. Yet how does Skinner explain a symphony?

The Judeo-Christian Cosmos
Every world view and every view of human nature must rest upon basic assumptions. Scientific humanism assumes ei-

ther that God does not exist or that he cannot be known. It also assumes something like potential omniscience for human science and human logic. Theistic thought assumes the existence of a holy, omniscient and omnipotent God, limitations of human science and the fallibility of human wisdom. If Christians are to understand scientific humanism, they must first recognize how it follows from its basic assumptions. Likewise, if scientific humanists are to understand the Judeo-Christian position, they must do the same; that is, they must ask what follows once one posits a holy, omniscient and omnipotent Creator.

The ancient documents of the tradition tell us that this Creator, having created all things for his pleasure, created Man *in his own image*. In contrast, then, to the "up-from-below" view of Man from scientific humanism, we are presented with a "down-from-above" Man.

What does it mean to be "made in the image of God"? To some it means that we possess certain attributes of God such as emotion, volition, intelligence and a sense of morality and ethics. Certainly the Scriptures portray us as having such qualities, including the ability to choose and a moral sense. According to the Scriptures we can make *some* real decisions (even though we may not be entirely free). In addition, we have had throughout our history a sense of "oughtness," a sense of right and wrong.

Others view the meaning of the phrase "in the image of God" differently. While acknowledging that the documents as a whole attribute such qualities to humanity, they suggest (and I believe that they are right) that the phrase has more to do with our function on earth. Like God we are to rule. "Let him have dominion over" the created order, God is heard to say in the beginning of the book of Genesis.

But from this lofty position of supremacy Man sinned and fell. In that fall he was both morally and mortally wounded. Sin had warped his personality. But it had done more. It had alienated him from God and distorted his relationship with creation. He now had to earn his food by painful toil. Sin also impaired (though did not destroy) his ability to think and to make decisions. More serious still, sin, like a disease, not only made him mortal but made it impossible for him, in spite of his best resolutions, to refrain from sinning. And in this sense too we see him as a "down-from-above" Man. We also see in him the shattered image of God.

Such are the brief opening chapters in the drama of our history. The millennia that followed represent the slow unrolling of God's plan to provide the means of our redemption.

For the Jews the redemption story is still not told in its completeness. They await a coming Messiah and are bewildered by the endless suffering of their people. To some of them the establishment of Israel as a modern state represents at least a part of that redemption, and, or so it is said in private, the redemption will not be complete until the boundaries of the modern state are such as are described in the books of Moses—that will mean the whole city of Jerusalem and a good deal of the territory over which so much controversy now rages.

Other Israelis deplore such a militaristic focus and the methods that go along with it, some because of liberal political views and others for religious reasons. The latter call for repentance before God, a return to the teachings of the Torah and prayer for the coming Redeemer King and Messiah. Some of the most heart-rending modern literature comes from the pens of Jewish writers like Elie Wiesel who give a sense of the incredible pathos, the agonized questioning about the Messiah who has still not come.

For Christians, the arrival of the prophet and rabbinical teacher Yeshua of Nazareth, commonly referred to now as Jesus, represents the great turning point in world history. His arrival was the cause of the tragic division between Judaism and Christianity, though it is interesting to note that it was not the Jewish nation as a whole who rejected Jesus. After all, the early church was composed largely of Jews, followers of the prophet Yeshua, whom they saw as Messiah and Lord. But it is time that we turned back to look at certain basic ideas of the Judeo-Christian tradition. We must look at its distinctive view of Man and Man's destiny.

Down-from-Above View

First, let me talk about Man's destiny. Both the Jewish and the Christian Scriptures view the events of history eschatologically. That is to say, they view all events past and present in the light of the termination of history. Human history— at least this phase and the present form of it—is to end. History is under the control of God. While we may not understand all his actions and purposes, he has declared his intent to return as Christ in power to supervise the liquidation of the present order. The graves will open and the sea will give up her dead. All wrongs will be dealt with. The secrets of our hearts will be laid bare. The standard by which we all will be judged is that of the holiness of God himself.

Earth and heaven will then be destroyed to give place to "a new heaven and earth wherein righteousness shall dwell." While humanists express the understandable human longing that a nuclear disaster will be avoided so that evolution and education may eventually perfect us, Christians look up, anticipating the return of One who has the sovereign right to dispose of human history.

So much for humanity's destiny. What of its distinctives? In what does the Judeo-Christian perspective see our greatest glory?

In the Judeo-Christian view our glory does not lie principally in our creativity or the architectural splendor of our civilizations. Instead everything springs from the "down-from-above" view of humanity. The noblest efforts of Christians and Jews have arisen from the idea that, however mean and humble, however unattractive and despised another human being might appear, we must remember we are dealing with someone created by God, in his very image.

Wherever this idea has prevailed—and the terrible sins of Jews and Christians alike make it clear that the idea has not always prevailed—we can discern the fruits of what I call *a high view of Man*. Among Jews and Christians there has always been a minority of people whose lives have been governed by this principle.

Their lives have had an enormous impact. Think of the names of the great London hospitals or those of many other great cities—St. Thomas's, St. Bartholomew's and a whole string of other saints—reminders that these hospitals are monuments to a high view of Man. The poor and the suffering had to be sheltered and healed *because they were made in the image of God.*

Let me make myself clear. I am not attempting to vindicate Christians so much as to look at the effect of an idea—the idea that human beings derive their importance from their high origin and high destiny. And the influence of that idea has spread into society generally. Many of the social attitudes we claim as enlightened and moral came from this source. It remains a powerful reminder of a specific view of human life in the remarkable work of Mother Teresa in Calcutta.

Malcolm Muggeridge writes of her, "I raised the point as to whether, in view of the commonly held view that there are too many people in India, it was really worthwhile trying to salvage a few abandoned children who might otherwise be expected to die of neglect. . . . It was a point, as I was to discover subsequently, so remote from her whole way of looking at life that she had difficulty in grasping it. The notion that there could be too many children was, to her, as inconceivable as suggesting that there are too many bluebells in the woods or stars in the sky. . . . To suppose otherwise is to countenance a death wish. Either life is always and in all circumstances sacred, or intrinsically of no account."[6]

But the question may come, What about slavery? Moses did not abolish slavery any more than St. Paul did. But even the Mosaic laws were by contemporary standards unusually enlightened in the treatment of slaves. But let us look again at the question. How did the overthrow of modern slavery come about?

In the Western world there were two sparks to the abolition of slavery, one in Britain and one in America. In Britain the active agents were a group of people known to history as the Clapham Sect. This handful of wealthy Anglican evangelical pietists devoted their fortunes to the education of the children of indigent miners and to the campaign to abolish the slave traffic through the agency of the parliamentarian William Wilberforce. (Curiously the abuses of child labor in England had previously been done away with through the influence of another pietistic Anglican, Lord Shaftesbury.)

In North America the abolition of the slave traffic began through the efforts of the Quaker John Woolman. Woolman was an extraordinarily gentle person who traveled incessantly on horseback, pleading the rights of Indians and intervening to prevent local wars and uprisings. But his greatest contribution was to visit Quaker settlements where by gentle persuasion alone he induced most Quakers who owned slaves either to free them or to grant them freedom on the death of their current owners.

In each case the underlying view of Man was the high view I have mentioned. And the motivation driving the men and women who espoused the causes I have mentioned was that of delivering others who, like them, were made in God's image.

Where Are We Going?
Proponents of both theism and humanism face the question of how to cope with the terrible possibility that efforts to prevent a nuclear holocaust will fail, as I believe they ultimately will. And time is not on our side. The solutions that humanists such as Skinner and Koestler have suggested to control or to correct the evil in mankind have no hope of being realized in our lifetime. One is an impossible Utopian dream robbing us of our dignity to tame our evil. The other is a hope in biochemistry which, for all our advances in brain science, remains in the realm of science fiction. In

spite of the genuine love of mankind that humanists obviously have, if solutions to the grave problems of human
nature must devalue or "dehumanize" people so radically,
I think it is fair to call their view the *low* view of Man.

How then do I as a Christian face the question of nuclear
war? I believe that all the films designed to impress on us
the unspeakable horror of nuclear war still can only portray
that horror inadequately. I believe that the God who controls human history may yet postpone the horror, but only
for so long. It has to come, and I suspect it will come sooner
rather than later, in spite of all our efforts to stop it. When
it comes I shall not be exempt from personal suffering. It
would be nice to be killed in the first searing flash. But
having thought about it, I am also willing to survive, be it
for a few minutes, a few hours or to face a prolonged and
lingering death.

Why? Because I would not be a lone survivor. I would be
surrounded in all probability by unspeakable distress, and
I would wish to do what little I might, even if it were only
to minister words of comfort and hope. People are worth
suffering for. They are that valuable.

My own hope lies in a new heaven and a new earth,
however foolish that may appear to others. But my hope
does not merely comfort me personally. It gives me joy in
doing what others might regard as hopeless and pointless.

In conclusion my thoughts return again to Arthur
Koestler, whose obituary I read in the March 15, 1983, issue
of *Time*. Koestler was a vice president of EXIT, a British
organization making available information to enable British-
ers to die painlessly and with dignity, if they so chose.

Koestler himself was seventy-seven and suffered from

leukemia and Parkinson's disease. He and his third wife made a suicide pact and died from an overdose of barbiturates, sitting together companionably in two armchairs. I suppose that from Koestler's point of view they were undergoing self-administered euthanasia.

His story symbolizes for me the consequences of two views of Man and of history—the humanist and the Judeo-Christian view. Somehow I feel that the view I espouse is the healthier and the nobler view. But what matters most is whether it is a correct view. And I have no doubt whatever that it is. I am therefore prepared to live and to die by that view and to worship alone that God who made me in his image.

TWO

THE MISSING ELEMENT IN PSYCHOLOGY

If we do not understand what a car is, we will have a miserable time trying to fix it. If I think a car is a permanent shelter, I might replace its wheels with cinder blocks to make sure it stays in one place and doesn't roll around. Or I might take the motor out so there will be room for more people.

This is absurd, you say? An incorrect view of a human being will lead to mistakes that are just as absurd. Differences between humanistic and theistic views of Man are relevant to clinical psychiatry and psychology. If humanists are correct about Man, certain therapies will be more appropriate to "fix" broken people than others. If theists are correct, what is appropriate and what is inappropriate will differ. If, as I suggested in the last chapter, the humanistic view (which supports most contemporary psychological theories) is inadequate, we would expect to find gaps precisely where theism provides answers. This is indeed the case.

The missing element in much counseling today is still the religious. Human beings are essentially religious. If, as I suggested in the last chapter, we are made in God's image, then we are made for fellowship with him—and this is the essence of religion.

Sigmund Freud was right to help us remove the taboos that surrounded the topic of sex both in light conversation and in serious study. It is now time that the taboo about religion also be removed. Although attitudes are beginning to change, as evidenced by the publication of such books as *The Road Less Traveled* and *People of the Lie* by M. Scott Peck, that taboo still exists.

I was taught as a resident in psychiatry that I must never allow a patient to talk to me about religion. The reason? Discussions of religion raised by patients usually represented a resistance to the psychotherapeutic process. Religious themes were antitherapeutic. They were the client's escape route from the medicine of the therapist. I came gradually to understand that though resistance to truth can take a religious form, it often is, in fact, psychiatrists and psychologists who are threatened by such topics. Many create barriers of resistance to them, anxious to avoid them for neurotic reasons of their own.

Two Religious Encounters

Let me illustrate the importance religion can have with two encounters I had early in my psychiatric career. During my first year as a resident I met Jerry, a young man who was sent to the mental hospital where I worked because he had a psychopathic personality. The son of a Pentecostal pastor, he was always getting into trouble with the law. No doubt he was reacting to his background. There had been family problems which had influenced his view of Christianity. Jerry was also extremely intelligent. His IQ tested out at 145.

As we talked together during one session, the issue of guilt came up. "I suppose your father must have taught you that there was some sort of answer to guilt," I said.

"Yes," he responded, "I would like an answer to that guilt. I would like to be forgiven. But for me to be forgiven there has to be some Cosmic Forgiver, and I don't believe he exists. I only wish he did." This spoke to me of the reality that human beings are essentially religious. Here was a man groping for an essentially religious answer for his life.

A year or two later I had an encounter also described in *The Masks of Melancholy*. I was in a general hospital when Howard was admitted and diagnosed as suffering from a psychotic depression. Though my supervisor was well versed in all sorts of approaches in dealing with human problems, he came to the conclusion (like I did at the end) that perhaps this man needed medication. So we gave him both antipsychotic and antidepressant medication. For weeks there was no improvement. Then we administered ten electroconvulsive treatments. Still nothing happened.

Then one day he and I were together, and one of those mysterious doors opened in which you find yourself facing somebody, naked spirit to naked spirit. He began talking about having drunk a bottle of beer when his doctor said he shouldn't because it would aggravate an ulcer he had. This was weighing him down enormously, out of all proportion of course to its real seriousness.

A more significant problem for Howard, at least one that we more readily recognize as serious, went back to World War 2. He had avoided enlisting, yet many of his friends had gone and some of them had been killed. This was weighing on him hugely.

"What about forgiveness?" I asked him.

"I want it so *bad.*"

"What's your religion?"

"Russian Orthodox."

"And what does your priest say about how you get to be forgiven?"

"He doesn't talk too much. We go to confession."

"And what does that do?"

"I don't often go."

I groped for words. "But if you do go, why would God forgive you?"

"Because Christ died. He shed blood."

"So?"

"But I'm too bad for that."

Unaccountably I grew angry. No logical reason. It just happened. "What d'you mean you're too bad?"

His voice was rising like my own. "I don't deserve ever to be forgiven."

"You're darn right you don't!"

He looked up at me surprised. "I can't be a hypocrite. I gotta make amends."

It may be hard to believe, but I found my anger increasing. "And who d'you think you are to say Christ's death was not enough for you? Who are you to feel you must add your miserable pittance to the great gift God offers you? Is his sacrifice not good enough for the likes of you?"

We continued to stare at each other, and suddenly he began both to cry and to pray at once. I wish I could remember his exact words. There's something indescribably refreshing about the first real prayer a man prays, especially when he doesn't know proper prayer-talk. As nearly as I can recall he said something like this: "God, I didn't know. I'm real sorry. I didn't mean to offend you." More sobs, tears, running nose. I passed him a box of Kleenex. "God, thank you. . . . It's amazing. . . . I didn't know it worked like that. . . . I thought . . . but, God, I don't know much. . . . Gee, God, I don't know how to say it. Thank you. Thanks an awful lot. Gee, God, *thank you.*"

I prayed, my normal fluency a little hampered by his emotion, while he mopped up his face with Kleenex.

His eyes were shining and he shook my hand. "Thanks, Doc. Thanks a lot. How come nobody ever told me before?"

During the following week I deliberately refrained from doing more than bid him, "Good morning, how are you?" each day. I wanted to let others record his progress. He had believed that his bowels were rotting away, a traditional symptom in a depressed person. He had also been paranoid, feeling that various people were out to get him because he was so bad. The nursing logs indicated that these things were rapidly disappearing.

The notes on his chart read, "Remarkable improvement. No longer seems depressed. Paranoid ideation not expressed. Making realistic plans for future."

We took Howard off all medication at that point. Then a week later he grabbed me and said, "Look, I've got to talk to you, Doc." We went to my office and the first thing he said as he sat down was, "It's as though all my life I've been blind, Doc. Now I can see." He hadn't heard any evangelical phraseology and didn't know that he was quoting from a hymn. Here was a man who was essentially a religious being. He was no different from other beings because human beings are religious.

For weeks we had been groping for an answer for Howard and had been skirting his essential problem. We had worked endlessly without meeting his need. The key to curing everybody who is depressed and paranoid is not necessarily for them to learn about forgiveness of sins. Howard's was an exceptional case. But it brought home dramatically to me that indeed we neglect a real element in human beings when we evade religious issues.

If we are dealing with something which is fundamental and basic to human nature, then some psychiatrists and counselors will find areas where they cannot be effective. One area concerns the sense of purposelessness so common today in society. Another is the use of coping resources, which counselors and psychologists are forever trying to teach their clients. Some people are able to utilize them, while others, however hard we try to give them coping mechanisms, never catch on. And sometimes I suspect there are religious reasons for their inability.

Irrepressible Religion
There is evidence of the religious nature of human beings

in primitive tribes as well. I have had contact with a number of primitive tribes. I have also read many anthropological studies of these tribes. And I have yet to come across an a-religious tribe. We are arrogant when we say, "Aha, yes. That's because they're uncivilized." We display the arrogance of our a-religious, technologically advanced civilization. One reason people in the West tend not to be religious may be that we have relegated religious questions to religious specialists. (Primitive tribes have their own experts— shamans, witch doctors.) But many experts and religious specialists in the West, ashamed of their field, tend to remove religion from the people rather than bring it to them. Our church structures symbolize a system that relinquishes responsibility to the priest or pastor.

And this has been unfortunate. Exposed to the sophistication of seminary, priests and pastors grew disdainful of the primitive Scriptures toward which they had once entertained a dutiful but uninformed respect. And under the guise of being now better informed, they tore the vitals out of them and presented a mutilated corpse instead of a living body of truth. Congregations, at first bewildered, eventually grew bored. By and large they still are.

There has, of course, been a specific discrediting of religion and of religious beliefs in the West. Scientific humanism has not found God necessary as an assumption to explain the universe around us. That notion has crept insidiously into our educational systems. In universities some who teach science courses react against their own religious backgrounds and inflict science as an antireligion on their students. In so doing they inflict their emotional hang-ups on their students. Or it may be that the mere emphasis on scientific discoveries and an everyday awareness of how useful technology can be causes God to shrink and grow pallid in the minds of Westerners. Science has turned us into magicians.

Yet now I see in the psychoanalytic movement, and in many other movements in psychology, religious elements arising within secular institutions. I suppose the elements must satisfy religious aspirations, cravings or instincts in the community the institution serves. The world without God, created in the West during the nineteenth and twentieth centuries and based on the Enlightenment, has produced a vacuum which is now being filled in many ways—some of them profoundly unhealthy.

I was first alerted to this many years ago when I was working with primitive tribes in South America. Reading anthropology, particularly field literature dealing with actual tribes, I came across an interesting paper from West Africa. An anthropologist there was studying high-school students who had been taken out of their tribal settings and exposed to British education. In place of tribal traditions they were taught physics, chemistry and other sciences. Their tribal beliefs were not deliberately lampooned or made foolish, but the underpinnings of the students' beliefs were removed. As they studied biology and evolutionary hypotheses, the world of their tribal mythology grew less real to them.

None of this was too surprising. But what interested the anthropologist was a sudden and widespread outbreak of primitive forms of witchcraft throughout school systems in West Africa. It was witchcraft unrelated to the customs of the tribes the students came from, even though each tribe practiced specific patterns of witchcraft. It was new, their own creation. His explanation was very simple. Something had been taken away that was important, and something more sinister and pathological had taken its place because the emptiness had to be filled.

Four or five years later I found myself in Buenos Aires, Argentina, which at that time had about seven and a half million people. At the center of the city I found a big bookstore with foreign sections. When I found the British books, I was astonished to find two long shelves filled with different paperback books published on witchcraft.

I pulled them out and began to read them. I noticed that most of them had been written in the preceding ten years when religion in Britain was perhaps at its lowest point. Into that vacuum had moved the occult. Later I learned from friends in England that witchcraft was indeed a serious concern in Britain. Witch covens were performing ritual murders. They were desecrating churches and stealing the symbols of their worship. As in West Africa, the unsatisfied hungers created by secularization had to be satisfied in more bizarre ways.

There was a spiritual vacuum in California in the sixties. A powerful movement arose promoting the freedom of promiscuity, preaching that we should make love not war. Then among the hippies arose the astonishing phenomenon of the Jesus people who embraced a puritanical abandonment of these things. No drugs. No booze. No sex (except in marriage). They would perform the marriages themselves and tell the couples they should stick together.

They even attempted to deal with homosexuality. They married off homosexuals to members of the opposite sex and supported the couples with prayer during their first attempts at copulation, which goes against all counseling and psychiatric principles. But for a while they were able to make a go of it. The success was even written up in journals.

Ultimately it failed, however, because it lacked a number of elements which are essential for the ongoing religious life of any group. It lacked authority structure—older, wiser people who carry the traditional knowledge and help the younger people on. Without these elements it disintegrated though its effects are still being felt in southern California. And in any case, the phenomenon clearly demonstrates the compelling yearning we share for the religious. For the phenomenon of the Jesus people was more than a puritanical reaction to hedonism. It was a manifestation of power.

In more recent years we have seen the rise of innumerable cults. Hare Krishna, Moonies, Baha'i and Bhagwan Shree Rajneesh became household words. Again we see flourishing cults as a symptom of a society in search of a meaning and purpose not supplied by the secularized West.

A Substitute Religion

Loosely organized as it may be, the human potential movement is likewise a substitute form of religion. Paul Vitz does not refer directly to the movement in his book *Psychology as Religion,* but the movement would fall clearly under his critique. Back when he wrote his book in 1977 what he termed "selfist psychology" was just coming into vogue. By this he meant psychology that emphasizes realizing one's full potential as a human being. He singles out Erich Fromm, Carl Rogers and Abraham Maslow as the gurus of the selfist movement. Many people were stimulated and refreshed by these authors, as I was when I read them. Underlying the movement was the doctrine of the total acceptance of the client. Here was a certain freedom from stuffy thinking and a healthy desire to help people without judging them or condemning them. A flood of literature followed—Eric Berne's *Games People Play,* Thomas Harris's *I'm OK, You're OK* and others. When orthodox psychoanalysts and orthodox behaviorists throughout the West began lapping up Transactional Analysis (TA) and abandoning their former disciplines of behaviorism or psychoanalysis because it was the trend, Vitz saw this as contributing all the more to the utter selfism of society.

Underlying the refreshing freedom was something we failed to notice, something more sinister. If I am interested primarily in me, if I have an undeniable right to realize my full potential—then logically my neighbors must take second place. My needs will take precedence over theirs whenever the two conflict. I would be loath to admit this. But logically it follows. The other person is devalued. I am number one.

This essentially selfish and competitive conclusion was perceived not only by Vitz but by writers and teachers within the movement. And by the end of the 1970s a number of popular books made it explicit. In these books the philosophy Vitz had called selfism openly became me-first-ism. While the "virtue" of me-first-ism was not acclaimed by the movement as a whole, the expression certainly represents a logical conclusion from its most basic tenet—I have the right to realize my full potential as a human being, in my sexual practices, in my ambitions and in every other way. This philosophy ends up deifying the individual.

Yet even deifying the individual does not satisfy religious cravings we all have. Interestingly, the human potential movement now is embracing Oriental mysticism, importing ideas from the East. Children in classes in California are being invited to lie on the floor when they are six or seven years old. Under the drugging voice of the teacher they are asked to imagine that the sun is up there, that they are rising, rising out of their bodies to the sun until they are out of sight of earth itself where they can absorb more and more of the sun, until they come back into themselves having become great, having become part of the universe. The movement is not merely a psychological movement. It is the West absorbing the East and struggling in the vacuum of religiouslessness for an answer which the East has been trying to find for centuries.

The monolithic resistance to religious ideas, once so much a part of the human sciences, is giving ground. Fascinated by whatever is new, psychologists and psychiatrists in increasing numbers are embracing the New Age. Holistic counseling has now come to mean counseling that embraces insights from the Orient. Naturalism is giving place to a quasi-religious monism. All is one, and in oneness with the All lies power.

The New Age psychologist believes that our yearning search for meaning can only be met as each of us emerges from the cocoon which currently imprisons us. We need a transcendant experience, an experience of oneness with It, an experience which will lift us out of self-doubt into channels of the powerful resources of the universe itself, of all being, of everything that is. What began with the deification of the self, has now become a deification of the All.

New Age advocates, then, are telling us to seek experiences that will expand our consciousness, enabling us to enter a new stage of being. Once sought through mind-expanding drugs (as people like Timothy Leary and Aldous Huxley urged) these states are now produced by techniques such as est (Ehrhardt Training Seminars) and, more recently, Forum. Douglas Groothuis describes a typical session.

In the est experience several hundred people are brought together for two successive weekends of marathon sessions designed to help them get "it." During the sessions they are confined to their chairs for long hours without note-taking, talking, smoking, clock-watching or sitting next to anyone they know. Minimal food and bathroom breaks are strictly observed.

Each of the sixteen-hour sessions is led by a trainer who berates, taunts and humiliates the crowd by insisting that their lives don't work. The sustained intensity leads many to become sick, cry or break down in some other way. That's the goal.

Through the agonizing hours of torture the tears turn to insight and the sickness into enlightenment. The participants are told, "You're part of every atom in the world and every atom is part of you. We are all gods who created our own worlds." Eventually the people—at least some of them—claim to get "it"; they experience enlightenment and oneness.[1]

And by making this quasi-religious leap, adepts become part of a new humanity, forerunners of a quantum leap in evolutionary development. If the old scientific humanism was optimistic, the New Age psychology is infinitely more so.

Similar borrowing from Eastern mysticism can be detected in meditation techniques and techniques of guided visualization, and a revived interest in the writings and concepts of Carl Jung. However, Jung, whatever may be said for and against his views, made it clear that not all the strange traffic with the symbols which come to us from our racial heritage represents good. Some traffic can be pathological and dangerous.

It is at this point that the hopeless naiveté of the New Age movement becomes apparent. Issues that Christian (and in particular Roman Catholic) theologians have debated for centuries are ignored. And with the arrogance of the half-literate we fail to see the monumental nature of the philosophical assertions we embrace, lightly dumping naturalism, deism, existentialism and theism, and cheerfully accepting monism. And why? Basically because it is exciting.

But then most food, even poisoned food, can seem exciting to starving people. So new power techniques are hailed with joy by the hungry psychological dabblers of the New Age. Members of the clinical professions have become sorcerer's apprentices, little knowing what they are playing with.

But whether Christian misgivings on this score are justified or not, it is becoming plainer and plainer that secular, nonreligious answers cannot be found to human yearnings. Belatedly, and in increasing numbers, psychologists and psychiatrists are turning to find religious answers to fit their patients' and clients' needs. There are still large sectors of the clinical professions uninfluenced by either the human potential movement or the New Age development within it. Some, more aware than others of the danger and inappropriateness of pretending to understand religious issues, invite people trained in religious disciplines to collaborate with them.

Here, too, there are pitfalls. In some cases pastors, priests and rabbis are given a certain amount of psychological theory and training to aid them in this collaboration. Curiously (so arrogant are we of the psychological sciences), we rarely invite *them* to orient *us*. In any case, the typical result is that psychological specialists in a hospital environment generally overimpress the religious specialists with their awesome clinical knowledge.

I suspect many of them would deny my assertion. But clinically trained pastors I have observed seem to have experienced little of the powers of the world to come in their own lives—too little to resist the lure of new techniques. I suspect they moved into psychology because they sensed a lack in their own ministries. But all that happens in psychological settings is that they seem to minister clinical comfort or challenge, only now in religious language. (And in religious settings they begin to minister the insights of psychology with theological authority.)

If you think I am despising their contribution, you are wrong. All I am saying is that in importing religious professionals into the clinical setting we have not really got to the root of the difficulty. We have not changed anything—unless it is an inadvertent dilution of theology. We psychologists and psychiatrists remain blind to the true nature of Man, and powerless to meet some of his deepest needs. In an attempt to benefit from the insights of religious specialists we have merely clothed David with Saul's armor.

With other religious specialists, psychiatrists in particular have a "hands off" policy. We show witch doctors more respect than pastors or priests. I have known Indian shamans and medicine men invited into psychiatric settings to help Indian patients with psychological problems. The psychiatrists in charge usually have no belief in the supernatural. But they have observed that the medicine man's methods work where modern psychiatry fails to. How they work would be interesting to discuss, but crowded schedules and half-digested meals leave no time for the most important discussions. The success, we say, is simply a matter of communication within the Indian culture. Simply? What goes on in Indian cultures? Communication among whom? Shamans' methods work (up to a point) not only because they communicate well within the Indian culture, but because some of them are in touch with power.

Once again we see that psychological specialists recognize the need for religious help. And once again the basic problem is being evaded. Is Man only a marvelously complex but closed system? Is behavior programmed, programmable and determined? Or do influences from Beyond interfere? What *is* the universe? What is Man? If he did come down from above, if he is a damaged image of the one Creator God, then this fact is supremely important.

Power

I said that New Age devotees (like certain witch doctors) are fascinated by powerful techniques. No one who has studied them seriously will doubt the reality of the power in the techniques. But in discussing the world view of the New Age I asserted that it was monistic. The picture at this point becomes more complex then. In chapter one the issue lay between (naturalistic) humanist and theistic understandings of Man and the universe. Now a third world view has been added—a world view that asserts that God is everything and that Everything (including ourselves) is god.

At first the view might seem not too different from theism, but a moment's thought will reveal how widely disparate it really is.

Theism sees God as a person, monism as an abstract sum of the parts. In theism, individuality and personality are important. To know and to be known are high values. In monism your ultimate goal is *un*knowing, the loss of your passions, your pains and even of your identity as you merge into the peace and serenity of the All. But Oriental considerations of this sort do not wave banners or march in the van of New Age psychology lectures. Underlying inconsistencies tend to be ignored. We are into clinical effectiveness, not philosophy. And power is power.

What does history tell us about the confrontation between the Judeo-Christian tradition and spiritual power? Much every way. You see power, *spiritual* power, in the classical struggles between the prophets and the sorcerers, between a Moses and the magicians of Egypt, a Daniel and the astrologers of Babylon, or a Joseph and the wise men of Pharoah's court. And Yahweh's power always wins.

The Scriptures recognize a primal and a subsidiary source of power. First, there is Yahweh, the Creator of all, from whom all things and beings come and by whom they all consist. Then there are fallen angelic beings, banned from his presence by reason of their wicked rebellion. Milton paints vivid word pictures of their fall. They are the "principalities and powers" of the air, purveyors of temptation, tragedy and deception, still wielding and even offering to men and women the powers they embezzled from heaven.

Because the ultimate source of power is and can only be one, manifestations of power, whether from its principal and original source or from the rebels who absconded from heaven with large quantities of it, will have the same basic characteristics. Demonic power is nothing more than divine power corrupted. Water does not cease to be water and may still look like, feel like and even sometimes taste like pure water when it is dangerously polluted. So devilish miracles, visions, dreams and so on may be very similar in type, but terribly different in their ultimate effects on human beings. The similarity will deceive "even the very elect." Satan will appear "as an angel of light." And whereas God's power will be redemptive, vivifying, cleansing, freeing and restorative, hell's will be progressively enslaving and end in death and destruction.

For let us admit it, the Judeo-Christian tradition is steeped in, nay *based on,* historical incidents involving supernatural power. Because we are Westerners we have tried to hang on to the "essence" of the tradition by demythologizing it. In so doing we have castrated it. Many Christians and Jews, even those who profess to be fundamentalists, would prefer to be thought of as scientifically sophisticated than narrow and bigoted. And the flight from the charge of bigotry can involve spiritual emasculation. Many Christian clinicians have been rendered spiritually impotent and spiritually in-fertile. For it is all too possible to be a theist intellectually and a naturalist in the way one lives one's life and exercises one's profession.

Indeed the terrible hunger that drives starving Westerners

in a frantic search of what naturalism has robbed us of, has progressively emasculated Christianity and Judaism. The only power we know is political power. Suddenly all over the world, Christian missionaries are faced with an increasing tempo of demonstrations of supernatural power that can no longer be explained away. And unlike Moses, Daniel and the apostles, most missionaries have no weapons to fight them with. Churches have stopped believing in divine power, paying only lip service to it. So they no longer can call on it in an hour of need. All they can do is warn us away from the dangers of getting too close to anything miraculous. God may be all-powerful, but it is the Devil we must really look out for!

Reared in the social and religious climate of "science," it is understandable that Christian and Jewish psychologists, while professing to believe in divine power, are by and large depending in their everyday practice either on techniques based on naturalistic assumptions, or are drifting into playing with fire. They have always had some ability to help, but they are as far as ever from getting at the root of human needs.

Many of us in psychiatry find the issues I raise threatening. Most of my professional colleagues avoid them, telling patients who raise them that they are resisting the help being offered to meet their "real" needs. Psychologists need to start asking: Do I have some problems with religious issues? What is my religious background? What was I taught as a child? How did it affect me? And how am I feeling about these things now? Psychologists who are interested in what is important to the client, as Carl Rogers would urge us to be, will find that in many marriages and human interactions religious conflict is to be found. Therapists will never fully understand the conflicts unless they are prepared to at least acknowledge their ignorance and face their own unconscious fears. Only then can constructive help result.

Mind and Body

The title of this book is *Putting the Soul Back in Psychology.*[2] But what is *soul?* Or better, what is *mind?* For in the human sciences, as distinct from theology, it is mind that fascinates us. There is something else we need to look at when we ask the question: What is man? This is the unity of our nature. Christians are as guilty as humanists of propounding unbiblical ideas about the different parts of a human being. This is because most of us possess a muddled mixture of Greek and Hebrew thought which we have inherited through Plato, Aristotle, the Gnostics, Thomas Aquinas and the philosopher Descartes. We have divided the human being up into a less important physical part (body and brain) and a more important immaterial part (mind and soul). We have made the matter even more complicated by discussing the "tripartite man" allegedly found in Scripture and neatly sectioned into three: body, soul and spirit. Please understand that I am not denying that terms such as *soul* and *spirit* are found in Scripture and much less that they are important. They are both. So are such terms as *mind, heart, will.* The question to be resolved is, What are the relationships among them all?

It would take too long here to examine the way each term is used throughout Scripture. But we can look at one or two facts. First, the terms mentioned, if we examine them in their contexts, have a certain amount of overlap. While they are far from always being interchangeable, they are sometimes so. Second, Scripture seems to conceive of a human being as a whole and not as a creature of divisible parts. We are not meant to have body and mind split up any more than soul and spirit. The doctrine of bodily resurrection should make it clear that we are and always will be bodily creatures.

What we have inherited from the Greeks is a wrong way of perceiving the relationship between mind and body, exalting the one and playing down the other. For in doing so, quite apart from denigrating bodies which Christ has sanctified, we have fallen into the trap of comparing things that cannot be compared. We are guilty of what some modern philosophers would call a category error, a mixing of apples and oranges.

To compare mind with body is like comparing music with the pianist's fingers. "What matters is the *music!*" we cry. Of course. But no fingers, no music. Clumsy fingers, bad music. Weak fingers, feeble music.

We are, perhaps, groping with ideas beyond our grasp. Let me attempt another analogy. We talk about "mind over matter." If we mean by the expression that we should not always give in to our physical weaknesses and cravings, the saying is a good one. But if we mean that there is a sort of wraith-like part of us—the *real* us—called mind that controls the solid part of us called body, we are liable to be confused.

Descartes in his sixth meditation sought to clarify the issue. The self, he decided, was lodged in the body as a pilot in a ship but was more important than a mere pilot. "I am not only lodged in my body as a pilot in a vessel but . . . am very closely united to it, and, so to speak, so intermingled with it that I seem to compose with it one whole. For if this were not the case, when my body is hurt, I, who am merely a thinking being, would not feel pain, for I should perceive this wound by the understanding only, just as the sailor perceives by sight when something is damaged in his vessel."[3] Ultimately, however, the mind was distinct from the body. This view which Descartes expounded gave rise to the term *Cartesian dualism.*

Descartes is aware of his dilemma. If mind is other than body, it must have some intimate connection with it. But how to describe the connection? He resorts in the end to anatomy. "In examining the matter with care, it seems as though I have clearly ascertained that the part of the body in which the soul [a term Descartes used synonymously with *self* and *mind*] exercises its function immediately is in no way the heart, nor the whole of the brain, but merely the most inward of all its parts, to wit, a very small gland which is situated in the middle of its substance and which is so suspended above the duct whereby the animal spirits in its interior cavities have communications with those in the posterior."[4] The mind, in a word, is found inside a gland, a gland in the brain, a gland which influences parts of the brain and body by *animal spirits,* "material bodies of extreme minuteness" moving very quickly "like particles of flame."[5]

I cannot do justice to Descartes' struggle to understand the nature of the human psyche. But clearly he struggled, as we all struggle, to comprehend things immaterial. Our souls do not in fact reside in the pineal bodies inside our skulls. Our minds do not flit from point to point inside our brains and bodies. The attempt to compare mind and body is doomed to failure from the start because of the category error I referred to earlier. One can only compare a thing with something else in the same category. You cannot discuss which is the more important, the color purple or a pound of cheddar cheese, nor whether the sound of middle C has greater significance than the amount of money you have in your bank account.

Function and Matter

The nearest we can get to describing the relation between mind and body is to consider matter in relation to function. A car runs. A machine works. An orchestra plays music. The relation of mind to body can be compared with the relation between the working of a machine to the machine itself or the relation of the music to the orchestra.

What do psychiatrists think of when they talk about mind? Usually they think of a bunch of bodily functions. I remember. I am conscious. I am aware that I am *me* as distinct from *you*. I feel emotions—anger, sadness, joy. I think, that is to say, I reason. I make decisions. Because these things I do (that is, being conscious, being aware of my identity, remembering, feeling, reasoning, deciding) seem to hang together, I include them under the term *mind*.

But notice. Mind is a group of functions, a group of bodily functions, functions not merely of my brain but of my body as a whole. Take my emotions, for example. As I step off the curb into the path of a car, I hear the screech of brakes, an angry hooting of a horn. I jump back. A car window rolls down and a man screams obscenities at me. How do I feel? Scared. Angry. But what do these feelings consist of? My heart is going *bump, bump, bump* in my chest. My face has turned white. My palms are wet and my fingers are shaking. I feel a little dizzy. All these things—beating heart, white face, sweaty palms, trembling fingers—are bodily sensations, sensations arising from what my body is doing. The bodily sensations I experience I call feeling scared or feeling mad.

Admittedly, my brain probably orchestrated this set of sensations I call fear, so that my brain organizes what my body does. Long ago William James suggested that we do not cry because we feel sorry but that we feel sorry because we cry. In the same way there is truth in the suggestion that my heart does not beat because I am afraid but that my fear consists of a beating heart and trembling fingers.

So I insist that mind cannot be compared easily with body unless we recognize that it belongs to a different order of reality. Mind is not a thing so much as an "ing"—a feel*ing*, a remember*ing*, a know*ing*, a think*ing*, a decid*ing* and so on. Mind is what body does; in fact it is what body goes on doing all my life, even when I am asleep.

So to ask, "Where is mind?" is rather like asking where the concerto is when the orchestra has stopped playing. Mind, in one sense, isn't anywhere. Like an idea, it is not limited to a particular time or place.

Now if mind is a function of body, it will seem clear that malfunction of my body can lead to malfunctions of my mind. Therefore "mental" conditions may perhaps have a physical explanation. Or can they? The question is not so simple. In saying that mind is a function of body, we are using an analogy. The analogy is helpful, but it will have limitations. Clearly it is our daily experience that mind affects body just as much as body affects mind. If I have a toothache and have not slept for three nights, my bodily state will induce a mood of gloom that cripples my patience and my concentration alike. Bodily ills do in fact lead to mental distress.

Alternately, if by use of my mind I discover that I am facing trouble (like losing my job, for instance), I might suffer physically. I might lose my appetite or develop a peptic ulcer. It would seem that the mind-function model may oversimplify matters. At any rate it must be clear to us that it is just as true to say that matter influences function as to say that function influences matter, or, in simple terms, body affects mind just as mind affects body.

What practical effect does all this theorizing have? Let me give one example: mental illness. If what I have suggested about the unity of human nature is true, then I think we must come to a conclusion that may shock some. Mental illness is a bodily illness. Remember what I said about the piano? Weak fingers—feeble music. I believe the same is true for mental processes.

Having said that, let me immediately hedge it about with qualifications. I am not suggesting we stop counseling and merely dispense medications. To continue my piano metaphor, there are any number of reasons for feeble music besides weak fingers—lack of practice or improper instruction are just two possibilities. A purely physical cause may not be behind the effect, but it may. And the role of the doctor is in fact to make the proper diagnosis of cause so the proper cure may be administered.

Too often, however, Christians fear the use of physical therapies to counteract severe mood disorders. Yet scientific evidence is mounting to show the effectiveness of antidepressant medications and of electroconvulsive therapy in such treatments. Research is also helping us understand more clearly what physical effects these have on neuro-chemistry to affect our moods and emotions so positively.[6]

The key to all of this is a thoroughly biblical perspective. It unlocks help for troubled people, fearful people, sick people, angry people, depressed people and sinful people. If our task is to help people become whole, we must begin with a correct view of what whole people are.

THREE

WHEN CHRISTIANS ADOPT SECULAR VALUES

The church is fascinated with counseling. Its seductive lure has captured pastors, professors and the people in the pews. Ironically, while most psychology has little to do with religion, religion can hardly seem to get enough of psychology.

There are dozens of books by dozens of Christians on dozens of topics ranging from coping with stress to understanding how you were raised as a child to getting along with your spouse. Quotations from psychologists illuminate sermons once laced with biblical texts. And hundreds of pastors are moving into pastoral counseling or social work.

It's amazing to find how many counselors are former ministers. Why this trend? Why this appeal? Where does it come from?

A Love-Hate Relationship

At the same time, many Christians fear science. As a first-year psychiatric resident sitting in an adult Bible class in a church in Winnipeg, I squirmed under a long tirade by a visiting Bible expositor (did he really not know I was there?) about the evils of psychiatry. Rather pompously he told us that one could be a Christian. One could be a psychiatrist. But one could not be both a Christian and a psychiatrist at the same time. Not ever. Occasionally I still hear such remarks, but they are growing fewer.

Why this love-hate relationship between Christians and science? If science "discovers" something that threatens Scripture or, which is much more likely, that threatens our favorite interpretation of Scripture, then science becomes the Enemy. Parents protest the way it is taught in schools. We busily create Christian schools and Christian universities for which, embarrassingly, we need to import Christian professors trained in godless universities. On the other hand, if science discovers something that supports our favorite interpretations of Scripture, we discard our hostility and hail science as the latest and most reliable champion of the faith. After all, if science proves the Bible, the Bible must be true.

Most of us understand little about science, have too great a respect for it and overestimate its power both to undermine and to build up our faith. Science has little power to do either. It is true that some teachers of science use "scientific" arguments against faith, just as some Christians use scientific arguments to "prove" the faith. But teachers of science and Christian apologists are human beings, and it is their human insecurity which sometimes is at work, not their scientific aptitudes.

Science is simply a useful way of looking at certain problems. It is limited in scope. It cannot bring about world peace, remove death or discover God. And while its application may add to the available supply of goods and services, it can do little to see that they are equitably distributed.

Despite these limitations, the tendency among most Christians is to glorify the sciences. In the love-hate battle over science, love appears to be winning. And in particular the psychologies fascinate us. Counseling is in. Young men and women who study psychology are likely to get better paying jobs with superior kinds of churches and have better prospects for an ecclesiastical career. I do not say that such should be their motive for studying psychology. I am simply pointing out the way things are. Pastors are frustrated by the perplexing family problems their church members bring them. It is a relief to be able to turn to an expert, and it is only natural to feel that what the church needs is more psychology.

But we expect too much of psychology. And we do so in part because we have lost confidence in the Christian gospel, however much we profess to believe it. Consequently, we are too prone to pass on difficult cases to obliging counselors, social workers and psychologists without carefully considering whether we are doing so merely to get rid of a problem we ought to have been able to solve. There are times when pastors and elders should refer members of their flock to mental health professionals. But I have a growing fear of the role of psychology in the church and of its tendency to infringe on godly counsel.

The human sciences are still cutting their teeth. They are crowded with unproved (and sometimes unprovable) hypotheses and conflicting theories. Professional counselors, psychologists, psychiatrists and social workers can bring to their work a zeal for their particular beliefs which is more religious in character than scientific.

They are only human. Give a human being a little knowledge (especially if the knowledge enables him or her to belong to a prestigious group), and whether the knowledge is true or false you get converts full of zeal for the "truth" you have imparted. Pour gentle contempt on other schools of thought and their teachings and you will have them laughing with you.

But I would be doing the human sciences an injustice if I only painted one side of the picture. At the core of the movements, dedicated investigators carry out painstaking studies. During the last fifteen or twenty years, psychologists, sociologists and psychiatrists of various schools have been humbly learning one another's languages and paying careful heed to one another's results. Not all science is "science falsely so called."

Scientific truth, like any other truth, can be frightening. You have to follow facts wherever they lead you, and at times they may seem to lead you down dangerous byways. Christians and non-Christians alike find the process difficult, for, though investigation will threaten all of us at different points, it will threaten all of us equally.

Christians need have no fear of science provided we remember three things. First, scientists are merely investigating the laws of our Creator. They sometimes make serious mistakes in their investigations and arrive at wrong conclusions. But if they pursue matters far enough, they can only find truth, for truth is all there is to find. But because scientists make mistakes, all scientific conclusions must be tentative. Sooner or later the most unshakable and most firmly founded ideas crumble and fall.

Consequently, it matters little whether science supports Scripture or not. If today's science opposes, we need not fear, because today's theory will be replaced by another tomorrow. By the same token, it is unwise to rejoice in science's support of Scripture. Who are scientists that they presume to "confirm" the Word of the living God?

Finally, science is only one of many ways of discovering truth and has serious limitations. It becomes dangerous only when we worship it, that is, when we assume it is the high road to all understanding. It can offer us no help with life's deepest questions: Why do I exist? Why is there a universe? Does life have any meaning? How can we determine what is important in life?[1]

The Greener-Grass Syndrome

In chapter two we looked at the religious gropings of the human sciences. But now we are considering the lure with which psychology attracts rabbis, priests and pastors. What really accounts for it?

Well, as we have seen already, the social sciences represent more than science. They represent a contemporary philosophy. And contemporary philosophies have always appealed to those religious professionals whose guilts and griefs have never been satisfactorily assuaged, who have never personally tapped a vein of spiritual satisfaction and power. Historically, whenever philosophy has disagreed with theology (as each new philosophy has), theology has tended to trim her sails to the philosophical winds of the day. Theology's most monumental work, Thomas Aquinas's never completed *Summa Theologica,* represented a kind of accommodation of Christian thought to Aristotelian philosophy.

It would be interesting to know what made him give up. Almost every biography tells the same story. For years, in accordance with Aristotelian thought, he had been working out a theological system in which Man has no direct experience of immaterial reality—and therefore of God. Hence his need to produce proofs of God's existence. Shortly before his death, however, he had such an experience himself—and promptly stopped writing. He had tapped the vein I spoke of a moment ago. "I can do no more," he told a friend. "Such things have been revealed to me that all I have written seems as straw, and I now await the end of my life."

We fail to learn from what happened to Aquinas. Theology can never have done with her flirtations with philosophy. The twentieth century began with widespread interest in a book written by a fascinating philosophical maverick, William James. It was called *The Varieties of Religious Experience* and consisted of twenty lectures, originally delivered as the Gifford Lectures on Natural Religion in the University of Edinburgh. The lectures represented an attempt at a psychological understanding of religion. It is still a widely quoted classic.

To his contemporaries James seemed to be the greatest American genius since Jonathan Edwards. He was, in the words of one writer, "a major philosophical planet who whirled on his own axis and drew all of the other pragmatic luminaries into his powerful field."[2] Having begun his professional life as a chemist, and having proceded via medicine to psychology, he wound up at Harvard as a philosopher.

There is a certain irony in the fact that jaded religionists looked to him for enlightenment. His excellent summary of true religion[3] makes much that passes for it pallid by comparison. And while he did not profess either "popular Christianity" or "intellectual theism," James clearly saw that understanding religion was no substitute for "living religion." A point would come where science "must drop the purely theoretic attitude, and either let her knots remain uncut, or have them cut by active faith." Science, as science, had too many unresolved problems of its own to pontificate on religion.[4]

A further irony lay in the fact that it was William James who invited Sigmund Freud to visit North America, chairing his opening lectures on this side of the Atlantic. Perhaps this very sponsorship secured for Freud a receptivity he never enjoyed in Europe. At any rate psychoanalysis grew and flourished following Freud's visit. Along with other social sciences, not only as sciences, but as a way of looking at Man and at life, they have slowly become accepted as essential to the life of Christians and the church. History has repeated itself.

When I practiced psychiatry I saw many pastors in my office. I learned of their doubts, fears, despairs and sense of frustration. I also met many social workers, psychiatric nurses, psychologists and full-time counselors who had once been pastors. Seminaries may be full, but once again, where do the graduates wind up? And why? People who want to help people need two things—a profound understanding of the deepest needs of the human heart and an ongoing experience of having their own needs met. And churches and seminaries are producing too few such people. We have a form of godliness, but have denied its power. Those who grope soon look wider afield. Many wind up around the skirts of the psychological sciences.

But there is another reason for our fascination with psychology—a very human reason. There is great satisfaction in sitting with somebody and being wise. Such a statement may make some people angry. "After all," they might say, "are we not giving of ourselves in counseling, trying to help others overcome their problems? And here you claim that counseling is an ego trip." If your training was in theology or religion, you may one day be haunted by a subtle fear that you really don't have much of value to offer people. The fear commonly arises from a lack of true spiritual power in your personal experience. To you it may seem that Scripture or perhaps God has not been effective at addressing the tough areas of human existence. Maybe there is something more useful, more helpful. Maybe it can be found in the psychological disciplines.

Unfortunately, this is often how our inner feelings, as distinct from our outward professions, go. Partly it is the grass-is-greener-on-the-other-side-of-the-hill syndrome. Theology was once firmly stated to be the queen of the sciences. But no longer. Most people are unimpressed by your studies in theology or that you are in a religious school. They may react politely to the information, but they do not feel you have something which is of infinitely greater value than what the human sciences have to offer. And you begin to share their feeling.

In spite of my serious charges in the first two chapters, I cannot deny that the human sciences have something important to offer, even though in their teachings I am beginning to see too many old things rehashed with a new twist. Perhaps we have exhausted the potential of this area for solving the human dilemma. And certainly for too long we have been ignoring something which is of greater importance.

When I was practicing psychiatry I never found my identity in my profession. That is, psychiatry was something I did rather than something I was. I don't know when that dawned on me, but I realized that I was primarily a follower of Jesus, a follower who happened to be practicing psychiatry. I was not despising the discipline nor the training that had been given to me. I threw my whole heart into the work I was doing. Nevertheless, I never lost my identity as a Christian. Rather, it has grown with the years.

I hesitate to be personal in this area because it is such an intensely individual matter. But too often, I feel, we find our identity outside that of being a follower of Jesus. Pastors and priests, like psychiatrists, find their identity in their job, their role, rather than in their relationship with God. We look to our background or our achievements or, in this case, our profession for our primary self-concept. If you doubt this, imagine quitting. Is not your first thought, "But what would I *do?*" And the result is that we are impoverished. We are poorer. We have turned our backs on the mighty resources that are available to us in our profession or other role.

Recently I was reading through Matthew in my devotions. I was trying to follow Ignatius of Loyola's suggestion to as we read imagine as vividly as we can the settings, the scenes, to feel the breeze and feel the sand under our feet. And again emerging from this Gospel I saw a man whose greatness has grown with me over the years. A man whom I still yearn to follow. A man who astounds me. A man whose stature grows continually in my eyes. When I think of myself as in some sense an ambassador of this Christ, I am astounded that I, being what I am, could represent him and who he is.

Personally, I envy those who can study theology. I have read some of the standard theologians, but I don't have the opportunity or the training of many others. Yet such biblical training is valuable because it opens for us the doors to all of life.

The irony of this situation is that while I long for more of it, pastors and flock alike are neglecting the queen of the sciences in favor of bankrupt human sciences. Once again, I do not dismiss what the human sciences have to contribute. But as I pointed out in chapter one, they are deficient not only in failing to deal effectively with the human problem, but in failing to see its essential nature. Though they give us valuable insights of which we should avail ourselves, they are unable to offer more than a partial solution to the dilemma we find ourselves in.

Christians in counseling must be equally wary of the determinism in psychoanalysis and behaviorism, as of the radically different New Age techniques. They must be careful not to allow themselves to react to their fellow human beings on the assumption that they can be conditioned, controlled or directed inevitably by applying certain laws or principles or techniques, any more than they should be exposed to dark power. Both are antithetical to a Christian view of Man. And ultimately they represent techniques of diminishing returns.

You may say, of course, that you see little evidence in contemporary society that the Judeo-Christian tradition offers any greater hope. My whole point up to now, however, has been this: Christianity has not been tried and found wanting—it has been found but not really tried, even by the churches. Only an emasculated, gutless travesty of it has been tried.

The rise of pop psychology and the human potential movement causes me even greater concern than the older disciplines—not only because it has infiltrated modern psychology but because, more surprising yet, it has infiltrated the church. One would think that these psychologies were poles apart from evangelicalism and fundamentalism. But, amazingly, large segments of the church have swallowed them whole.

Many Christian counselors would deny this. But consider what evangelical publishers have done in recent years. They have seen that money can be made out of this approach to counseling and have baptized it, personalized it, put a few verses of the New Testament over it and sort of reinterpreted it in biblical language, without changing its substance. Without realizing what they're talking about, without realizing what I see to be its inherent great dangers, they have provided evangelical bookstores with hordes of books offering shallow reflections on crucial questions.

Christian Clubs

Certainly psychology has done some good. For one thing, psychology sometimes draws attention to biblical principles we have neglected or been blind to. But its teaching has come to many pastors as a tremendous relief for the wrong reasons. Frustrated because they don't seem to get anywhere unless they become the kind of entrepreneurs who build large churches, write best-selling books, develop a TV ministry or have buses importing hundreds of Sunday-school children, the new psychology has come to their rescue. It has given them something modern and relevant to preach to their people, something that touches their lives. Unfortunately, having sometimes begun by unwittingly preaching a diluted gospel, they have, with the addition of psychology, wound up preaching a yet more diluted one.

Even evangelicals with a more comprehensive view of Scripture and a more comprehensive understanding of cultural trends have also been affected. Disenchanted, disillusioned and disappointed with their churches, they have suddenly found something here that they can do. Thus the great pastoral counseling movement was born. Over the last twenty or thirty years it has developed in unparalleled fashion.

The reason? There was a need for it because churches were not truly "churching." They had become Christian clubs, a place where Christians could feel reasonably comfortable, where things were run for them by a professional staff. They were being urged to be volunteers and do things like teach Sunday-school classes, but essentially they were led to feel that church should also be a club with a congenial atmosphere.

In that kind of setting an enormous number of human problems are not dealt with—wife swapping, adultery, homosexuality, to name only a few. Many Christians grappling with such problems sit quietly in churches not daring to open their mouths. Fellow church members treat them courteously. If some ugly problem breaks the smooth surface, it is dealt with quietly, discreetly. Offenders are shown out through the back door. On the other hand, if you make a million dollars (even if you've made it in an unethical way) and give a nice gift to the church, then of course you are respected and regarded as one of the great men or women of God. You are contributing to the Christian cause and being very generous about it, and we won't concern ourselves with your business ethics. The tragedy is clear.

Pastors cannot possibly deal with deep moral problems because they are too busy running their staffs. They are run off their heels getting the club and its many programs going and keeping them all going. They have too much work to do currying favor with the power group in the church and getting more new people to join. I know this picture is overdrawn. Yet pastor after pastor says, "I just don't have the time to deal with these human problems." Thus the need for pastoral counselors.

More Than a Bandage

Yet I believe that pastoral counselors on the church staff represent a bandage approach to the problem. Obviously their appointment books are full, and any pastoral counselor will tell you he or she is needed. But when we look at the situation as a whole, we realize the problem has arisen because the church is not being the church. We have sold our birthright for a mess of pottage. Though it may be legitimate as a temporary solution to a church which is sick, clearly it is not the basic solution.

What is needed is an environment that nurtures others in the body, creating a context for a healthy church. Over the past thirty years a powerful and still-growing movement of home fellowship groups has revitalized the churches of a wide variety of traditions. Small groups have added zest to teaching, worship, prayer and evangelism, and have changed fellowship from an abstraction to a living experience. The proliferation of such groups reflects a deep hunger for intimacy that larger-sized groups cannot meet.

Some of the hunger arises from the very fact that church life is often one-sided. But it is aggravated by social problems created by urbanization, industrialization and technology. The intimacy of even the nuclear family is disappearing as divorce and separation take their toll and as TV sets suck into their devouring mouths the energies and affections we once reserved for real people.

For too long churches have been obsessed with bigness and growth, and too little aware of their depersonalizing dangers. Large groups can never be the seedbeds of healthy church discipline. If it is to be full-orbed, it must begin in the intimacy, concern and fidelity found in a small fellowship group.

Many books give practical instructions for forming and running small groups. My preference is for groups that are mixed in age, sex, educational and social backgrounds, that are integrated into a larger church fellowship and that are geographically based. But they will not come into existence easily. They call for thought, prayer and above all a thorough conviction about their place and value. What else can we say to inspire such commitment?

First, no awakening or revival makes an enduring impact on a society without them. Whitefield could probably out-preach Wesley and may have won more converts in his public meetings, yet Wesley influenced the course of British life more powerfully and for a longer period. The difference did not lie in the numbers of their converts but in Wesley's more thorough organization of his converts into *classes* and *societies.*

The classes, subunits of the societies, consisted of a dozen or so people meeting weekly with their leader to share their spiritual advances and setbacks and to reconcile quarrels and disagreements. The majority of conversions as well as the building of disciples took place in the classes.

In *Dynamics of Spiritual Life* Richard Lovelace mentions Count von Zinzendorf's "band system." The community of Herrnhut "was futher subdivided into group meetings for sharing, mutual correction and confession, and prayer. The band meetings made [free] use of lay leadership. . . . In many respects Herrnhut must be considered the most thoroughgoing and fruitful application of the principle of community in church history."[5] Not only were those with theological training or pastoral gifts involved in ministry, the whole church accepted its responsibility to counsel one another, to rebuke one another, to encourage one another and above all to love one another. Wesley's societies and classes had the same effect, reinvigorating the church in the midst of a hostile environment.

Second, small groups that meet in homes or on church premises can provide what may be the only realistic answer to the congregation's pastoral needs. No pastor, however gifted, can care effectively for more than thirty families. If they think they can, their delusion arises from their ignorance of the families' real sins and problems.

In his *Reformed Pastor* Richard Baxter left us an invaluable treatise on pastoral devotion, but its value lies precisely there—in its call to devotion rather than in its practicality. Baxter set aside many hours every week to interviewing families committed to his care. Yet to each family he could give only an hour or so twice a year. Baxter's ardor and commitment should stir us all to zeal, but his model is inadequate.

Third, and here lies the crux of the matter, Christian growth has to be learned. We cannot learn to love people unless we are close enough both for comfort and for inconvenience. Love costs. Growth in Christian love calls for interacting with unlovable Christian people.

Fourth, fellowship groups can become fertile soil in which new leaders develop and flourish. Whereas exclusive participation in large activities tends to infantilize and intimidate us, smaller groups entrust members with responsibility and give them confidence as they learn leadership skills because they are more tolerant of mistakes.

Finally, small groups provide the basic environment for training in godliness. Small group members have more opportunity to know one another. Personal idiosyncrasies and annoying habits do not take any longer to come to light than positive qualities. If fellowship is to remain warm and living, the negative traits have to be faced and dealt with.

Small fellowship groups will not guarantee these results. Small groups can be totally ineffective. They merely provide the logistical setting in which certain results can take place. But without the setting the results will almost certainly not follow.

Behind the structures must be a commitment to one another. I find constant references to this in Paul's letters. "Therefore encourage one another and build one another up" (1 Thess 5:11). "Let the word of Christ dwell in you richly, teach and admonish one another" (Col 3:16). There is a mutuality of Christian ministry. "Be kind to one another, tenderhearted, forgiving one another" (Eph 4:32). "If a man is overtaken in any trespass, you who are spiritual should restore him in a spirit of gentleness" (Gal 6:1). Paul was writing not to the leaders of the church but to the body of the church. The critical solution for the church now is what Lovelace would call the integration of the microcommunities with the macrocommunity of the church. With all the potential for small groups going wrong because of arrogance, enthusiasm or lack of training, there is also the potential for ordinary people to build up one another, to share together, to pray together, to worship together, to learn the Bible together. All this can then flow back into the macrocommunity to bring life to it, to bring a sense of community. This is how God intends deep healing to take place—in the body, in the fellowship, in the church. Let us likewise commit ourselves to it in his name.

FOUR

THE HUNGER
FOR THE HOLY

The best-known quote from St. Augustine is found in the first paragraph of the first chapter of the first book of his famous *Confessions:* "Thou hast made us for thyself and our hearts are restless till they find their rest in thee." So far in this book we have looked at whether or not Man has a religious nature and how the psychological community and the Christian community can nurture this. In this chapter I want us to look more closely at what this religious urge is, at what this restlessness is. I also want us to consider the kind of encounters with God that it can lead to. In particular I want to talk about what might be called close encounters of the holy kind.

It may seem that I have selected unnecessarily spectacular encounters with the divine. Spectacular they may be. But I have a reason for selecting them. As I examine them carefully I begin to discover important facts about the humans who have undergone such encounters—facts that are universal. The relationship between God and human beings, to say nothing of what we know about God, also takes on new dimensions.

Over a period of time it became progressively more clear to me in my psychiatric practice that Man is "homo religiosus." While I was careful not to take advantage of my position as a physician, nor to impose my religious convictions on vulnerable patients, I knew that many of them had profound religious concerns which they longed to share with someone they could trust.

The outlook of scientific humanism which has pervaded modern society has not diminished a longing for God. It has increased it. But now that the information about God is less available, that same longing seeks an outlet in disturbingly pathological practices. Just as men in prison or on long expeditions seek a sexual outlet in what has been termed situational homosexuality, so men and women around the world who have been robbed of access to or belief in their traditional religious practices turn to ugly and pathetic superstitions. People will always pay a price when that religious drive within them is stifled or frustrated. And in the wild potpourri of cults, new religions and the pop psychologies of the human potential movement, I see only evidence of people's hunger and thirst for a God they do not know.

The Holy

We human beings, whether we recognize it or not, have a yearning to know the Holy One. We may deny it. Our culture may rob us of any belief in its existence. Or our yearning may emerge in bizarre and sinister forms to mock us and lead us astray.

And the yearning, even if we are conscious of it, will be tinged with doubt. For somewhere deep within us we are aware of *das Heilige,* of what holiness is. And no matter what we say we believe in our heads, our hearts tell us (when we pay heed to them) that we are morally unclean. Much as we long to meet the Holy One, much as we recognize that he is our Heavenly Parent and his house our home, we know our filthy feet would foul his presence or else that his burning holiness would consume us.

There are then two problems if we are to meet God in a close encounter. If God is a Spirit, a Spirit who fills the universe and everything that might exist beyond time and space, how could a pair of human eyes ever see him? And if we are sinful and God holy, that is, if God is a fire and we are straw, how can it be safe for us to enter God's presence? The fact is that it is not safe. It is exceedingly dangerous.

I said at the outset that I wanted to talk about what I termed *close* encounters, extraordinary encounters. I shall not be referring to prayer, though this is one form of encounter. We do indeed enter the "holiest of all" when we pray. Yet even so there are degrees to which the immortal God reveals himself. On the one hand, Jesus (whom we believe to be God incarnate) could mingle with men and women without causing them any harm. On the other, when the veil that clothed his glory was torn aside on the Mount of Transfiguration, his disciples were filled with terror. Likewise today, from time to time men and women gain such a vision of glory that it fills them also with terror and wonder.

Dr. Rudolf Otto, theologian and philosopher, in his book *The Idea of the Holy* tells us that he ventures to write about the " 'supra rational' in the depths of the divine nature." God's holiness is not merely a form of supergoodness, of absolute purity—though it certainly includes both. It is the ultimate moral beauty of such infinite power and scope that it transcends all human understanding. It is least of all an abstract quality, something to describe in scholarly books or to flatter ourselves that we have a handle on it. It is the living God himself. Yet he can, and at times he actually does, communicate it—and himself—to us.

> Eternal light! Eternal Light!
> How pure the soul must be
> When, placed within Thy searching sight,
> It shrinks not, but with calm delight
> Can live, and look on Thee!
>
> O how shall I, whose native sphere
> Is dark, whose mind is dim,
> Before th' Ineffable appear,
> And on my naked spirit, bear
> The uncreated beam?[1]

According to Otto, a number of elements can be distinguished in men and women who have thus encountered

God. He vigorously denies Schleiermacher's assertion that these elements are mere extensions of those feelings devout Christians experience in their worship, feelings of awe and reverence, even of rapture. Otto sees these at best as analogies of what a close encounter with God is like.[2]

Otto uses, as C. S. Lewis in later years did, the term *numinous* to describe the quality of the fear that is experienced. The numinous experience is made up of an overwhelming sense of one's creaturehood, such that the subject experiences a "submergence into nothingness before an overpowering absolute might."[3] Other elements are what he calls "Mysterium Tremendum" in the face of "that which is hidden and esoteric, that which is beyond conception, understanding, extraordinary and unfamiliar."[4]

Otto elaborates on these and many more elements, but the question arises, Of what value is it to consider unusual experiences? What practical difference can it make in our lives and/or faith (or absence of faith)? Can it, as Aquinas hinted at the end of his life, contribute to our grasp of reality?

Earlier in this century God was under attack. The time came when he was briefly reported to be dead. But during the past half century he has in fact been trivialized, packaged for entertainment, presented as a sort of psychological panacea, a heavenly glue to keep happy families together, a celestial slot machine to respond to our whims, a formula for success, a fund raiser for pseudoreligious enterprises, a slick phrase for bumper stickers, and a sort of holy pie and ice cream. How impoverished this all is, how virtually blasphemous when compared to the experiences recorded in Scripture.

When John the apostle, slaving in salt mines on the island of Patmos, caught a vision of the glorified Christ, he fell at his feet as dead, so awesome was the sight.

When the prophet Daniel saw that same glory and heard words of thunder, such terror seized his companions (though they themselves saw nothing) that they fled. As for Daniel, he tells us, "My strength left me; I became a sorry figure of a man, and retained no strength. I heard the sound of his words and, when I did so, I fell prone on the ground in a trance. Suddenly a hand grasped me and pulled me up on to my hands and knees. He said to me, 'Daniel, man greatly beloved, attend to the words I am speaking to you. . . .' When he addressed me, I stood up trembling" (Dan 10:8-12 NEB).

When Job was caught up into the whirlwind to hear the words of God he said, "I have spoken of great things which I have not understood, things too wonderful for me to know. I knew of thee then only by report, but now I see thee with my own eyes. Therefore . . . I repent in dust and ashes" (Job 42:3-6 NEB).

If God is God, it is important that we know him as he is, not as we recreate him in our imaginations. It is important for us to know him as he is, for how can we speak to others of him when we have never trembled before his glory? Is it not possible that for all our biblical expertise and our claims about the Spirit's power, we still present a God who is small enough to fit inside our tiny brains?

Revealed in Symbol

Consider two passages from contemporary English litera-ture. Both are from novels, one a children's story. Each passage presents in allegorical form what I have been talking about. In both cases it seems the authors must themselves have encountered the numinous to be able to write as they do, though God is not mentioned in either passage. In one allegorical reference he is a mammoth butterfly and in the other the mythical god Pan. Yet each writer is really writing about the Judeo-Christian God and the effects of a close encounter with him.

The first passage is from Charles Williams's novel *The Place of the Lion.* Mr. Tighe, a collector of butterflies, early in the story sees the Great Butterfly, from whom all others have their being and to whom countless myriads of butterflies fly in great clouds.

Mr. Tighe was by now almost hanging to the gate, his hands clutching frenziedly to the topmost bar, his jaws working. Noises were coming from his mouth; the sweat stood in the creases of his face. He gobbled at the soft-glowing vision; he uttered little cries and pressed himself against the bars; his knees were wedged between them, and his feet drawn from the ground in the intensity of his apprehension.

Anthony moved and blinked, took a step or two away, looked around him, blinked again and turned back to Mr. Tighe. He was about to speak, but, seeing the other man's face, he paused abruptly. The tears were running down it; as his hands released the bars Anthony saw that he was trembling all over; he stumbled and could not get his footing upon the road. Anthony caught and steadied him.

"O glory, glory," Mr. Tighe said. "O glory everlasting!"

Anthony said nothing; he couldn't begin to think of anything to say. Mr. Tighe, apparently collecting himself, went an unconscious pace or two on, and stopped.

"O that I should see it!" he said again. "O glory be to it!" He wiped away his tears with his knuckles, and looked back at the garden. "O the blessed sight," he went on. "And I saw it. O what have I done to deserve it?"[5]

The second passage is from Kenneth Grahame's inimitable story *The Wind in the Willows,* a story about animals on the bank of the River Thames in England. A baby otter named Portly is lost. His parents are grief stricken. The two central characters in the story, the Rat and the Mole, spend all night looking for him. It was feared that little Portly had been swept over a nearby weir, and Rat and Mole make their way to the island just above the weir before daybreak. Light begins to dawn as they continue their search. But they find something else before they find Portly.

"This is the place of my song-dream, the place the music played to me," whispered the Rat, as if in a trance. "Here, in this holy place, here if anywhere, surely we shall find Him!"

Then suddenly the Mole felt a great Awe fall upon him, an awe that turned his muscles to water, bowed his head, and rooted his feet to the ground. It was no panic terror— indeed he felt wonderfully at peace and happy—but it was an awe that smote and held him and, without seeing, he knew it could only mean that some august Presence was very, very near. With difficulty he turned to look for his friend, and saw him at his side cowed, stricken, and trembling violently. And still there was utter silence in the populus bird-haunted branches around them; and still the light grew and grew.

Perhaps he would never have dared to raise his eyes,

but that, though the piping was now hushed, the call and the summons still seemed dominant and imperious. He might not refuse, were Death himself waiting to strike him instantly, once he had looked with mortal eye on things rightly kept hidden. Trembling, he obeyed, and raised his humble head; and then, in that utter clearness of the imminent dawn, while Nature, flushed with incredible colour, seemed to hold her breath for the event, he looked in the very eyes of the Friend and Helper; saw the backward sweep of the curved horns gleaming in the growing daylight; saw the stern, hooked nose between the kindly eyes that were looking down on them humourously, while the bearded mouth broke into a half-smile at the corners; saw the rippling muscles on the arm that lay across the broad chest, the long supple hand still holding the pan pipes only just fallen away from the parted lips; saw the splended curves of the shaggy limbs disposed in majestic ease on the sward; saw, last of all, nestling between his very hooves, sleeping soundly in entire peace and contentment, the little, round, podgy, childish form of the baby otter. All this he saw, for one moment breathless and intense, vivid on the morning sky; and still, as he looked, he lived; and still, as he lived, he wondered.

"Rat!" he found breath to whisper, shaking. "Are you afraid?"

"Afraid?" murmured the Rat, his eyes shining with unutterable love. "Afraid! Of Him? Oh, never, never! And yet—and yet—oh Mole, I am afraid!"

Then the two animals, crouching to the earth, bowed their heads and did worship.[6]

I hope I have made it clear that in both of these passages the encounter with the holy is dealt with in an allegorical form. Grahame is not suggesting that God has curved horns and a beaked nose, nor is Charles Williams portraying God as a gigantic butterfly.[7]

But earlier I asked the question how a human being is to experience an encounter with an invisible spirit-God. Both Williams and Grahame intuitively grasp the answer. We cannot see spirit. Yet God, who always is more anxious to draw near to us than we are to draw near to him, can, has and does reveal himself in symbolic forms, some that are simple and easily comprehended, and others that are complex and bewildering.

Yet whatever the symbolic form (readily understood to those of us who learn about the matter afterward) or however obscure, the impact on the individuals affected by it is always overwhelming.

The French philosopher Pascal left on record the fact that he had such an experience. But scholars are both frustrated and intrigued by his sparse details. With mathematical precision he records not only the date, but the precise times of its commencement and termination. But for the content of the encounter he leaves us one word only—"FIRE!"

Others commonly describe themselves as weeping, as experiencing an appalling loss of strength, as trembling, as experiencing a strange combination of joy and terror. At times, of course, God grants them experiences of him that overwhelm them with his love and joy and peace. But when his utter holiness is in view, they commonly suffer from an appalling sense of their own wretchedness and of their own sin.

Abraham Encounters the Holy

Let me turn now to some biblical encounters with the holy. The Judeo-Christian saga really begins with a man called Abraham. As we read Genesis we find that God is forever speaking to him. And on most of the occasions we are not told how, whether by an audible voice, a vision or merely by an inner conviction. However, on one or two occasions the account is specific and detailed.

In one incident, Abraham is groping for more assurance that God will fulfill his promise to give to Abraham the land where Jew and Arab are currently contending. In answer God tells him to bring animals and birds—a ram, a heifer, a female goat, a dove and a fledgling. The creatures were not to be offered as a sacrifice but were to be cut in half in accordance with local customs concerning the making of a contract.

The Bedouin practice in solemnizing an agreement was to separate the two halves of animals, leaving a path between them. To walk along the path between the slaughtered halves was to say, in effect, "May I be slaughtered and cut in pieces if I break this contract!" But in Genesis 15 Abraham was not expected to walk between the mutilated carcasses. The covenant that God was about to ratify was no human contract. Rather he was about to demonstrate to Abraham that his promise was every bit as solemn as any human contract. And he was to do so in a way that would deeply impress Abraham. God himself was to pass along the narrow corridor between the animals.

So Abraham procured the animals, slaughtered them and spent the rest of the day driving carrion away from the carcasses as he waited to see what would happen. Then as evening fell, Abraham had his close encounter with God.

One translation reads, "An horror of great darkness fell upon him" (Gen 15:12 KJV), and another, "great fear came upon him" (NEB). At that point Abraham heard God's voice again, and in this case my guess would be that it was a solemn and audible voice. What we are actually told is that God revealed to Abraham the future history of his descendants including their ultimate possession of the land. But more was to follow. As the sun went down his startled eyes witnessed a smoking brazier and a flaming torch floating down the path between the slaughtered animals.

Smoke, fire and the light of a flaming torch—symbols of the holy. Yet Abraham would know with utter certainty that God was there in the symbols, and knowing, he would tremble. And knowing and trembling, he would find his fears mingled with joy and wonder.

The first time I experienced a close encounter with God, I began to understand the power of symbols. One day I had been preoccupied with one of my personal problems. For various reasons, some of them having to do with the way I was brought up, I had all my life found it difficult to *receive* love from anyone. Demonstrations of affection toward me made me feel awkward and uncomfortable. Although I had been aware of the problem for many years, I thought very little of it. The only matter that concerned me was my inability to experience the love of God. God's love was nothing more to me than an intellectual concept.

Then on the fourth anniversary of my father's death, as I thought about him and mourned his passing, I became peculiarly aware of my inability to know the love of my heavenly Father toward me. Throughout the afternoon I continued to reflect sadly about it, not because I had any sentimental desire to feel loved so much as because it seemed to me that I dishonored God by this peculiar quirk of mine.

That evening I happened to be praying with some of my friends in the living room of my home. My eyes were open, and I was fully aware of my surroundings when suddenly in three dimensions and full color I saw the arms and hands of Christ extended toward me. The effect was overwhelming. All strength left me, so that it was with difficulty that I remained kneeling. I began to sweat profusely and to tremble uncontrollably.

Strange as it may seem, I was fully aware that what I saw was a product of my own brain. I felt that God was, as it were, using my mind as a projectionist uses a projector. The hands I saw were not the real hands of Christ: They were weak and effeminate, whereas I knew that the hands should have shown the evidence of manual toil. They weren't carpenter's hands. They were pierced as tradition portrays them, in the palms, though the wounds should have been in the wrists, not in the palms, for the Romans used the wrists in that barbarous form of execution. Despite all these facts, I was moved in my depths.

It was hard for me to speak coherently for I wept and shook. The hands were inviting me to come forward and to take them in my own. But I was powerless to do so. My arms hung helplessly at my side. There was nothing in the world I would rather have done than to respond to the gesture the hands so eloquently portrayed. My arms were not paralyzed, but they might just as well have been, for I could not, in spite of the yearning that possessed me, move them a single inch.

While I said that I saw the arms and hands suddenly, I do not mean that they *appeared* suddenly. I had the strange impression that they had been there all my life, but that I was noticing them for the first time.

Brokenly I begged Christ to break down the walls I had built around me to protect me from the love I feared so much. And somehow the knowledge came to me that there would be no need for the walls to be broken down, but that little by little I would open myself to this terrifying love. And thus it has proved to be.

One could look at such an experience from many angles—psychologically, physiologically and so on. But I would like to focus on one, one that is important to us in understanding the revelation of God to Abraham. What I saw was a symbol, a symbol of a divine love I was invited to accept. I know that. Yet the awesome presence of God was there in a degree I had never known before. The invisible, eternal God manifests himself in symbols. Yet the symbols *are* his presence. Or at least they are the nearest expression of his presence we can know in our fallen condition. For Abraham it was a smoking brazier and a flaming torch. For Jacob it was a wrestling man. For John it was the awesome figure with feet of burning bronze, eyes flaming with fire and from out of whose mouth came a sword.

But there is one more close encounter I would like to look at before we conclude. And it deals with the most important feature of the human reactions to an encounter with the holy.

Holy, Holy, Holy

Isaiah tells us that when he was in the Temple in Jerusalem

in the year of the death of King Uzziah, he experienced a close encounter with the holy. To use his own words, "I saw the Lord seated on a throne, high and exalted, and the skirt of his robe filled the temple. About him were attendant seraphim, and each had six wings; one pair covered his face and one pair his feet, and one pair was spread in flight. They were calling ceaselessly to one another, 'Holy, holy, holy is the LORD of Hosts: the whole earth is full of his glory.' And, as each one called, the threshold shook to its foundations, while the house was filled with smoke" (Is 6:1-4 NEB).

Once again we see God present in symbol. We are not meant to understand that God sits in heaven on a throne which is approximately fifty times the size of an earthly throne. The throne Isaiah saw symbolizes God's awesome majesty and authority. Again, however enormous the figure that Isaiah saw—probably extending far above the Temple ceiling since the hem of his robe alone filled the Temple—it does not indicate to us the actual size of God who, if we must insist on thinking in spatial terms, fills heaven and earth. The seraphs in this incident actually proclaim that the whole earth is filled with his glory. Nevertheless, the awesome size of the enthroned figure would overwhelm Isaiah.

There were also the symbols of smoke (as in the case of Abraham and in other cases recorded) and, as we shall see shortly, of burning coals.

Nor are we meant to understand that seraphs are essentially six-winged creatures, though as a child I always, after reading this passage, thought of them as cute little six-winged things fluttering around the Temple fluting their treble praises to Yahweh. The actual description is quite different. However large or small they may have appeared

89

to Isaiah, they must have been awesome creatures. Such was the power of their thundering voices that the threshold of the Temple shook to its foundations whenever they uttered their adoring cries. And as for the wings covering their feet and their faces, clearly they betoken awe and deep humility before the figure sitting on the throne.

Their cry, "Holy, holy, holy" is of profound interest. Emphasis in Hebrew is conveyed by repeating twice the word to be highlighted, a device we sometimes employ in English. Jesus also emphasized a point with his "verily, verily," which we are meant to understand as, "What you are about to hear is utterly, utterly true."

What is interesting is that nowhere else in the Bible is any word repeated three times for emphasis, except in Revelation 4:8 which describes an almost identical scene. Thus the cry of the seraphs can only be interpreted as an expression of that which cannot be expressed, the ineffable holiness of God. Isaiah would feel the terrible weight, the scorching heat of the essential quality of the divine—a holiness that transcends all human understanding.

How did he react? In terror he cried, "Woe is me! I am lost, for I am a man of unclean lips and I dwell among a people of unclean lips; yet with these eyes I have seen the King, the LORD of Hosts" (Is 6:5 NEB).

We all know in an intellectual sort of way that to be in the presence of a holy God would make us conscious of our sin. We can even get some idea of the matter by imagining what it would be like to find ourselves, say, at a royal garden party, surrounded by impeccably dressed royal guests, while we were still unwashed and wearing the old, rough clothes in which we had just finished gardening. And if Rudolf Otto is right, the difference between that imaginary experience and Isaiah's encounter with God is not merely one of degree, but of a quality we could know by experiencing it ourselves.

Isaiah has an appalling awareness not only of his own sin but of that of his environment, the sin of the nation of which he is an integral part. "Woe is me! I am lost, for I am a man of unclean lips and I dwell among a people of unclean lips; yet with these eyes I have seen the King, the LORD of Hosts." His cry represents no ordinary conviction of sin, no ordinary remorse, but an unspeakable horror.

He needed no instruction from the seraphs nor any word from the throne. In a flash the reality was hideously clear. He knew the unknowable, was overwhelmed by the unutterable.

Yet God takes no pleasure shaking us like a dog shakes a rat, so that we fear for our very existence. It is just that he, being what he is, cannot approach us, being what we are, without this happening. Always his mercy finds a way to come to our aid and sustain us. If our agony includes, as it inevitably will, a crushing weight of guilt, he makes and indeed has made a way of cleansing.

Isaiah tells us what happened in his own case. "One of the seraphim flew to me," he writes, "carrying in his hand a glowing coal which he had taken from the altar with a pair of tongs. . . . 'See, this has touched your lips; your iniquity is removed, and your sin is wiped away' " (Is 6:7).

Isaiah does not tell us what effect the seraph's action had on him. My own experience under similar circumstances was of great joy and a sense of freedom I had never known before.

The Reminder

What profit is there in considering the nature of such encounters? Are they the experience of the few? Do they represent some exalted state that all of us should seek to attain? Are there rigorous disciplines to be followed so that others might likewise experience the holy?

Some mystics might answer yes, but I am not one of them. I believe that the experiences of the mystics, though they may have certain similarities, are not the same as those we have been considering. In every example I have given, the encounter came unsought, unbidden. Some encounters, it is true, took place during prayer or during the time of worship. But in no case was the prayer or the worship undertaken with any anticipation of what was to follow. In every case the Holy One himself took the initiative, to the shock, the dismay, the fear and the wonder of the worshiper.

So the question remains. Of what value is our consideration? Of what religious value can there be in what, after all, are the mere subjective impressions of a minority?

I mentioned earlier that we live in an age when God has been trivialized. From pulpits throughout the West and through an unprecedented flood of magazines and books, from radio broadcasts, bumper stickers and the slickness of cleverly orchestrated television programs we are subjected to a bombardment of God-the-convenience, God-the-cuddly-comfort, God-the-slot-machine, God-the-fast-food-merchant and the dial-a-prayer God.

The world clamors for God-the-Superpsychologist, for the God-who-can-make-us-slim-and-beautiful, and we package such a God for commercial distribution. Yet hidden within human hearts lies a mirror, a mirror in which we can see no reflection of our own faces, but the face of the living God. We need only to be awakened to his presence in that inner sanctum.

Some may discover that in the very descriptions I have given that their hearts confirmed the reality of such a God and of the solemnity and the marvel of the fact that he calls us to know him. We do not all need the terrifying experience of his close approach, but we do need to be reminded from time to time, if only through the experiences of others, about his dreadful majesty and his aweful holiness.

Let us then seek him with the aid of the Spirit and of the holy Word. Let us go to him in stillness, seeking that mirror in the deepest depths of our being, behind which this same God is waiting for us.

Notes

Chapter 1: More Human Than Humanists Know

[1]David Neff, "Who's Afraid of Secular Humanism?" *HIS* 43, no. 6 (March 1983).

[2]Arthur Koestler, *The Ghost in the Machine* (New York: Macmillan, 1967).

[3]G. K. Chesterton, *The Everlasting Man* (New York: Image, 1974), pp. 27-35.

[4]J. B. S. Haldane, *Possible Worlds* (Salem, N.H.: Ayer, 1928), p. 209.

[5]C. S. Lewis, *Miracles* (New York: Macmillan, 1947), pp. 21-22.

[6]Malcolm Muggeridge, *Something Beautiful for God* (New York: Image, 1977).

Chapter 2: The Missing Element in Psychology

[1]Douglas Groothuis, *Unmasking the New Age* (Downers Grove, Ill.: InterVarsity Press, 1986), p. 24.

[2]This discussion of mind and body is also found in John White, *The Masks of Melancholy* (Downers Grove, Ill.: InterVarsity Press, 1984), pp. 41-47.

[3]Descartes, *Sixth Meditation.*

[4]Ibid.

[5]Ibid.

[6]White, *Masks of Melancholy,* pp. 126-40.

Chapter 3: When Christians Adopt Secular Values

[1]A similar discussion of science is also found in White, *Masks of Melan-*

choly, pp. 57-60.

[2]Morton White, *The Age of Analysis* as quoted on the cover William James, *The Varieties of Spiritual Experience* (New York: New American Library, Mentor).

[3]William James, *Varieties,* p. 367.

[4]Ibid., p. 370.

[5]Richard Lovelace, *Dynamics of Spiritual Life* (Downers Grove, Ill.: InterVarsity Press, 1979), p. 166.

Chapter 4: The Hunger for the Holy

[1]Thomas Binney, "Eternal Light! Eternal Light!"

[2]Rudolf Otto, *The Idea of the Holy* (New York: Oxford University Press, 1950), pp. 8-9.

[3]Ibid., p. 10.

[4]Ibid., p. 13.

[5]Charles Williams, *The Place of the Lion* (Grand Rapids, Mich.: Eerdmans, 1933).

[6]Kenneth Grahame, *The Wind in the Willows,* pp. 117-18.

[7]William's allegory is actually somewhat obscure and convoluted, and demands an acquaintance not only with Platonic ideas but with Abelard and other medieval thinkers.